P

"*Passing on Curves* delivers a strong, necessary dose of the realities of growing up with hemophilia in the '60s and '70s, and the disastrous era of HIV-tainted blood products that followed. 'Real life' also happens to people with chronic blood diseases, of course; so AIDS and ankle pain from joint bleeds end up stirred in together with guns, children, parents, tigers, exes, and many adventures in this terrific stew of storytelling."

—**Ellis Neufeld MD, PhD,** *Medical Director, Boston Hemophilia Center*

"*Passing on Curves* is a beautiful book about life, loss, grief, death, hope, courage, and resilience. McLaughlin writes with great compassion, vulnerability and economy, and his stories are like polished jewels. I started reading it and couldn't put it down!"

—**Starhawk,** *global justice activist and author of* The Fifth Sacred Thing

"These stories are poignant, funny, outrageous, and deeply human. Craig McLaughlin is a fine and generous storyteller who inspires us to take risks, survive long odds, and re-create our lives and ourselves with meaning and love."

—**Ruth L. Schwartz,** *National Poetry Series-winning poet and memoirist*

"Craig McLaughlin is a fighter who eloquently holds love and hate, life and death, simultaneously. *Passing on Curves* teaches us what it is to be human."

—**Anne Hill,** *radio host and author of* When Dreams Go Bad

"This is an important book on many levels. McLaughlin's exploration of how forces such as shame and resilience shaped his own character offers lessons for us all. McLaughlin shows a great understanding of male development, working with shame on so many levels and healing it through telling his story. I want to share this book with my therapy clients. A brilliant book, by a heart-wrenching, seat-of-the-pants storyteller."

—**Sheila Rubin, MFT, Rdt/bct,** *co-creator of Healing Shame workshops*

Passing on Curves

While Death Rides Shotgun

Craig McLaughlin

Eli —
Nice to meet
a fellow memoirist!
Thanks.

HERNE

Copyright © 2015 by Craig McLaughlin

Published in the United States by Herne Publishing.

Herne Publishing
1300 Ordway Street
Berkeley, CA 94702-1124
www.hernepublishing.com

ISBN-13: 978-1-940462-03-5
ISBN-10: 1-940462-03-7

For Manya

Contents

The beautiful blue death spirit stays close to you at all times. Not your lover, not your chaperone. Neither your assailant nor your bodyguard. He doesn't feed you or feed on you, not even the way a butterfly sips from a flower. He just stays close.

I think perhaps he sings a little, sometimes. Or plays a blue flute.

—Ruth L. Schwartz
from "All the Bodies"

The author, approximately 15 years old, with Gretchen on Tiger Island

Foreword

IN THE MID-1990s, I SPOKE to high school classes about living with HIV in the hopes of dispelling the students' fears and prejudices. My strategy was simple: Put a face on the epidemic. Make them like me, because if they cared about me, someone who had contracted HIV through blood products, they might also care about the other victims, the marginalized ones.

It wasn't about me, or at least that was what I told myself. Then one question stripped me of that conceit. In a tenth-grade health class, a petite, brown-haired girl in the second row raised her hand and asked, "Have you thought about how you are going to tell your daughter? I am just wondering because my father died when I was three."

I paused before answering. My daughter was three. I was confident I would be there when she turned five, but I didn't know how much time we would have after that. I only knew I was having trouble picturing her after the age of eight. I couldn't project myself into a future that distant.

"I don't know," I finally answered. Then I asked, "Do you have any advice for me?"

The girl bit her lower lip. I imagined her herding her emotions into a pen built from her father's bones. There was only the tiniest quiver in her voice when she answered. "Pictures," she said. "Take lots of pictures."

Lots of pictures. But there are so few pictures that tell my stories.

I believe only three photographs exist of me with the big cats. Two feature me sitting in the grass with a young jaguar on a leash. Rolls of fencing and bales of hay surround us. In the background, Jeff, the Himalayan black bear, watches us from his cage.

The other photograph is yellowing, creased, and stained with something that looks like rust. I am inside the twelve-foot fence that surrounds a compound known as Tiger Island. I am perhaps fifteen. My brown hair is below my shoulders, so long it forms ringlets in the back. My clothes are of the period: early '70s, wide bell-bottom jeans and a yellow-and-brown zippered shirt made out of a ribbed knit. The outfit begs for a medallion of some kind, but only fools wear jewelry when socializing with tigers. If you have to pull away suddenly, you do not want to risk having a ring, bracelet, or necklace catch on a piece of fencing or, worse, on a claw or incisor.

I am seated on a chain-link walkway that spans the moat around Tiger Island, and I am reaching out to touch the wet nose of Gretchen, my stepfather's first Bengal. She is grown, weighing about a quarter ton, and I appear vulnerable, unable to run or leap backward if she lunges.

What the picture doesn't tell you is that I couldn't run—my crutches were just outside the frame. I was sitting because I couldn't stand. The photograph also doesn't tell you that tigers generally won't cross a bridge they can see through—they don't trust its solidity. I was on the bridge because it was the safest place in the one-acre compound, although if I could reach Gretchen, she could certainly reach me.

You see how it happens? I started writing about photographs and quickly lapsed into a story. A picture is not worth a thousand words. People will show a snapshot and think they've told their story. They'll look at a picture and think they've remembered an event, but perhaps they have forgotten the crutches just outside the frame. I worry that our ability to recall and relate the details of our lives begins to atrophy when we rely too much on photographs.

My daughter's mother is a shutterbug. So, when the student told me about losing her father, I knew my daughter would have hundreds of photos of me. But I am a writer and a storyteller. I am the sum of my stories, a golem built from the clay of memories, or at least from the grainy mud that remains after those memories have been watered down and contaminated by a fickle and overactive mind. If my daughter was to know me, really know me, then I would have to write down my stories. So, I started to put my life into words, and over many years they formed an accretion: stories of the stepfather who introduced me to wildness, the friend who introduced me to the fox demon, and the dog who introduced me to myself. Stories of lions and tigers and AIDS! Oh, my!

New drugs came along and HIV became a manageable condition, but I continued to write until I ended up with about 800 pages documenting my life. Then I split the material in two and shaped the first part into a coming-of-age memoir. It was partly a disability memoir, partly a story about my high school years on the tiger farm and my dysfunctional blended family, and partly a tragic love story. My intent was that the remaining material would eventually become a second memoir.

Then came the fateful invitation from Magdalena, a friend who knew some folks in San Francisco who produced a show called Fireside Storytelling. Six performers told ten-minute stories loosely related to a monthly theme. The theme for that month was "Regrets, I've had a few." Magdalena had been wanting to go for a while and was looking for company.

When it comes to culture, I have always been more inclined to be a producer than a consumer, so I pitched the organizers a piece called "Passing on Curves" about deciding to have a child when I was most likely dying, and sometimes questioning that decision. The piece was well received, and they invited me back the next two months. Three months into my new career as a storyteller, I was also performing in Oakland and Santa Cruz and had recorded stories for *Snap Judgment*, a radio show on NPR. More importantly, I had fallen in love with the form. I immediately began cannibalizing my memoirs for material I could shape into ten-minute stories. Curiously, the restrictive story structure gave me more freedom to say what I wanted to say than the longer forms of autobiography and memoir.

I am incredibly lucky: My daughter is now a young woman, and to my great joy and occasional embarrassment, I think she knows her idiosyncratic father well. If I had died when she was six or seven or eight, as I once expected, I would not have left much of a written legacy. It took me a long time to document my life, and even longer to find the format to say what I wanted to say.

I have many more stories, but if this collection is all I leave behind me, it will be enough.

And to the girl in the second row, I say: They are not quite what you had in mind, but here are the pictures.

Sorry it took so long.

Michael Bleyman, the author's former stepfather, with a baby jaguar

6

The Blue Flute

DURING A WRITING WORKSHOP a couple years ago, one of the participants looked at me—or maybe a little off to the side—and said, "I see you, Death. Don't think you can hide, because you can't. I see you skulking there."

Some people might find this disturbing, but unfortunately, this kind of thing happens to me a lot. My friend Laila often sees Death beside me, too, but she doesn't think of him as skulking. Once, she told me she saw him playing a blue flute. When my friend Ruth heard this, she worked it into a poem.

I have a memory that cannot be a memory. Maybe it's a dream or some kind of vision. I no longer remember how it first came to me. I am on a steel table, and people are poking me, prodding me. The steel is cold against my skin and everything hurts, even the bright lights and the loud voices. I miss the darkness and the sound of my mother's heart, not just the beating, but also the soft swoosh, the steady reassurance of valves opening and closing and opening again. The harsh light is not as bad as the needles, though, and worse still are the sense of violation and the awareness of something inside me I cannot name, some way in which I am broken. This isn't how it is supposed to be. This isn't how *I* am supposed to be.

My infant body is splayed out naked and defenseless. They have already cut away a piece of my flesh, and that would have been enough, but this is something more, something even they didn't expect. "This is my body," I want to scream. "You have no right to hurt me this way, to make me feel powerless and ashamed." I hear someone crying, and I think it is coming from me, so maybe I am saying just that, but without the words that will come later, after language, after a different kind of awareness.

They are doing this for my own good; they tell me that, or I know it somehow. This is how I survive, the only way I survive. And so I let go. Boundaries are a luxury I cannot afford. I let them in. I let everything in.

My mother went into labor on her twenty-third birthday. It was the Monday before Thanksgiving. Exhausted from ironing my father's shirts, she took something to help her sleep and went to bed. Around noon the next day, she deposited my older sister at a neighbor's and drove herself to the hospital. She wasn't sure she was going to make it, but she did. That was Tuesday. On Thursday they circumcised me, and then I bled and bled and bled. The pediatrician did not make it home to eat turkey and stuffing and cranberry sauce with his family.

After my poor little penis stopped hemorrhaging, the doctors told my parents the bleeding suggested a clotting disorder called hemophilia. Damage to blood vessels from a cut or an internal injury normally triggers something called the coagulation cascade, a series of interactions that join various proteins to form a clot. My body does not make enough of one of

8

those proteins, or what it makes is defective. The men in white coats who were circled around the steel table had no way to identify which factor I lacked, so they sent me home without a definitive diagnosis.

Hemophilia usually runs in families, but my family has no history of any bleeding disorder. My mother attributed my genetic flaw to studies she participated in when she was a nursing student and needed money, studies that required numerous pelvic X-rays. My maternal grandmother, however, favored a different explanation: My problem, according to her, was God's punishment for my mother's sinful ways.

Grandmother Judith, you see, was a nasty piece of work, but there seems to be a medical explanation for her, as well. And it may be from her that I inherited my stubborn insistence on living. As a teenager, she was sledding when a car forced her off the road and she slid headfirst into a tree. Doctors of her day could do little for a crushed forehead, so they put her in a hospital bed and waited for her to die. When she recovered miraculously, months later, she rose from her bed, brushed her bangs across her forehead to cover the scar, and went on about her life.

This is also something of a family legacy: hiding the scars.

My early life was a steady succession of bleeds. Some days, I would begin bruise-free, but then they'd start to surface, building slowly until they seemed to cover me. Hospital visits became more frequent once I started to walk. I would fall and bruise myself against the furniture, or I'd land on my jaw and bite my tongue. After one such fall, my mother watched in awe as a doctor with huge hands deftly tied a stitch in my tiny, two-year-old tongue. Afraid of triggering more bleeding, the doctor decided not to remove the stitch, and my tongue grew over it the way a tree eventually engulfs a nail. Perhaps with a normal tongue, I might have grown up to tell normal tales, but we'll never know.

One day, I tried to pull myself upright by grabbing hold of a rocking chair, but the chair lunged forward into my face and knocked out a tooth. My mother rushed me to the hospital, where doctors struggled to get the bleeding under control, giving me whole blood to replace what I was losing. My mother was not allowed in the room, so she didn't know until she got the bill that the doctors had been worried enough about the blood loss to order oxygen delivered. Losing a tooth could mean losing my life—that was a truth my parents lived with every day.

I lived with it, too. In my thirties, while visiting my in-laws, I was bored and started thumbing through their old set of the *Encyclopedia Britannica*. Under the heading for *hemophilia*, the encyclopedia said the life expectancy of a newborn hemophiliac was twelve years. I was curious, so I checked the publication date. It was 1957, the year I was born. There was something reassuring about reading this in print, about finally having a number. No one ever told me as a child that I was likely to die young, but I knew. Perhaps I gleaned it from the looks, tones, and body language of my parents and the long string of medical providers who tended me. But I think I knew it that day on the steel table, under the bright lights. Only two days old and already I was dying. I came back, have continued to come back again and again, but I returned from that first crossing with a new companion.

He has been at my side all this time. He was there the night I knocked out my tooth. He was there the day I found out the blood products I used to treat my hemophilia had given me HIV. He was there the night my daughter was born with her umbilical cord wrapped twice around her neck, and the day a surgeon removed almost fifty cancerous nodes from my wife's left side and shoulder. Most recently, he was there as my liver slowly deteriorated because of hepatitis C.

I wouldn't say we are friends exactly, but we have reached some kind of understanding. We respect each other.

He stays close. When I am worn out from all the effort I put into staying alive, he sings to me gently, reassuringly.

And sometimes he plays a blue flute.

A Different Kind of Injury

AN OLD CLASSMATE SENT ME a friend request on Facebook a couple years ago and followed up with a little note, something to the effect of, "Craig, I am so sorry I gave you such a hard time in high school." A lot of people picked on me in school because I was smaller, younger, and more sensitive than most of my peers—and I was on crutches a lot. People tripped me, called me names like cripple and faker, and ran off with my crutches. But I didn't remember this guy, much less being bullied by him. I think like most people he didn't understand the four major types of trauma I experienced growing up with hemophilia. So here they are:

Number one WAS the ankle bleed. For most of my childhood, this was the most common type of injury. Ankle bleeds seemed to happen spontaneously. The hemorrhaging could be in the soft tissue around the ankle or in the joint itself. Joint bleeds are among the most painful injuries known and require treatment, while back then muscle bleeds were left to resolve themselves. Every bleed started out as a muscle-tissue bleed in my mind and only became a joint bleed when I admitted that I couldn't take the pain anymore—and that always made me feel like a failure.

When I had a joint bleed, the doctors would stick a needle into my ankle joint and draw out as much blood as they could. They would anesthetize me for the procedure, and I would wake in a hospital bed, my ankle immobilized in a knee-high cast. Being stuck in a hospital bed was never fun, but it did have a few advantages. I learned how to flirt, for example. If I talked to the nurses in a way that made them smile, they would let me stay up late and would bring me hamburgers from the cafeteria. A few days after an aspiration, the doctors would send me home on crutches. A few weeks later, I would return so they could cut off the cast.

Around the time I turned four, an orthopedist put a cast on my swollen ankle, and my heel began to hurt several days later. My mother was convinced something was wrong and called my pediatrician. He said, "He's just a spoiled little brat who wants to get his cast off." Then he prescribed a narcotic.

Several days passed before the orthopedist heard about my problem. He immediately cut off the cast and found a black, squishy spot the size of a silver dollar. The orthopedist was furious with the pediatrician. The orthopedist had put the cast on when the ankle was fully swollen, but once the swelling had subsided, the cast no longer fit. My Achilles tendon had tightened up, pressing my heel against the back of the cast, and pressure had formed an ulcer that extended to the bone. It healed eventually, but I was left with a permanent flat spot on my heel.

Number two was the mouth bleed, my arch nemesis. There are better treatments now, but when I was young and bit my tongue, the wound scabbed over but blood continued to ooze underneath, stretching the elastic scab like the skin of a balloon. The result was a clot the size and color of a blueberry. This had an upside: If a girl teased me, I could stick out my tongue, and she was guaranteed to run away screaming. For a young boy, this was like having a major superpower.

One evening, I was sitting on the kitchen counter, and when I slid down, I slammed my face against the corner of the dishwasher, driving my upper front teeth clear through my lower lip. It would have been a nasty-looking wound on anyone, but on me it was truly gruesome. My mother sent me to school, but the wound grossed out my teacher, who sent me to the principal's office with instructions to call my mother and have her take me home. My mother, however, told the principal, "If the teacher is squeamish, that's the school's problem, not mine."

The principal sent me back to the teacher, who returned me to the principal, who once more called my mother, who once more refused to come get me. The poor man, caught between two defiant women, parked me in his outer office until school let out. I was incredibly bored until I noticed a poetry anthology on one of the side tables. That was the day I learned to appreciate poetry, and I can still recite Carl Sandburg's "Fog" and Robert Frost's "Stopping by Woods on a Snowy Evening" from memory.

Number three: knee bleeds. These usually start in older kids. My knees were fine until high school, when I got run over by a llama on my stepfather's farm. The llama, which was aptly named Mephisto, saw himself as a family member, and he devoted much of his energy to finding ways to sneak through the pasture gates so he could hang out around the house. To the dogs, that meant he was fair game. One day, I was walking between the two barns when the llama turned the corner, running full tilt with one of the dogs in frenzied pursuit. The llama wasn't about to surrender and in such a narrow space a collision was unavoidable. As he barreled into my back, my right leg buckled and I screamed in pain.

My knee swelled rapidly, and everyone quickly agreed that I needed to go to the hospital. The docs treated me and after a few days sent me home to recover, even though I couldn't straighten my knee. The knee was still stiff a couple weeks later, when the electricity went out during a cold spell. I was living in a trailer with electric heat, and the loss of electricity meant the temperature was dropping fast in a room full of tropical fish and cold-blooded reptiles.

I wrapped my eight-foot boa constrictor around my neck to keep him warm and began hobbling around the room, bagging up my fish so I could move them to the main house, which still had heat. When I planted my good leg on a wet spot in the linoleum, the leg slipped out from under me. I instinctively tried to catch myself, shifting all of my weight, plus an extra forty pounds of boa constrictor, onto my bad knee, which collapsed underneath me.

I stayed longer in the hospital this time. After doctors got the bleeding under control, they put me in traction with a weight at the end of my leg to force it to straighten. After two weeks, I had full extension. The only problem was that now I wasn't able to bend my leg more than about ten degrees. I met with my orthopedist and a physical therapist before going home. The therapist wanted me to strengthen the knee, and she taught me how to tighten my quadriceps. Neither of them seemed concerned that I couldn't bend my knee, and I assumed the motion would come back on its own.

Months later, I still couldn't bend the knee more than twenty degrees. We consulted the orthopedist, and he quickly identified the problem: me. "This wouldn't have happened," he proclaimed, "if he had done the exercises I had prescribed."

I told him I had done everything they had asked, yet he all but called me a liar. When he left, I turned to the two residents sitting beside my bed. "He just told me to flex my quads," I sobbed. "That's all he said. I didn't lie. I did everything he told me." One of the docs looked over his shoulder as if to make sure his boss wasn't within earshot. "It's OK," he said, taking my hand. "We know."

You already know about the fourth kind of injury: being called a spoiled brat because my ulcerated heel hurt, being kicked out of class because the teacher couldn't look at me, being blamed for the fact that my knee didn't bend. These are injuries to the psyche. They are the result of being shamed. I could provide a lot more examples, like the doctor who spent all afternoon trying to get a needle in my vein, then said the problem was that I was pudgy, or the nurse who said that people like me should never be allowed to have children.

The classmate who apologized on Facebook couldn't have known that after years of walking the halls of medicine, I had been bullied by the best. By comparison, people like him—the baby bullies who prowled the halls of my high school, two junior highs, and three different elementary schools—were merely wannabes.

I never did answer my classmate's message, because I didn't want to hurt his feelings. I didn't want to burst his bubble. I didn't want to tell him how little he really mattered.

16

Playing by the Rules

I FIRST MET MICHAEL ALAN BLEYMAN in his office at the University of North Carolina. I noticed right away a strange fish on his desk. "That's George," said Mike. "He's a piranha." Then Mike explained that it was illegal to keep piranhas in North Carolina because if a pair escaped they might start breeding in one of the state's many rivers.

Mike was my mother's faculty adviser. My mother could almost instantly divide one six-digit number into another in her head, might have been valedictorian of her high school if she hadn't skipped gym class so often, and graduated Phi Beta Kappa from UNC after completing most of her courses at Harvard. Yet my father never understood why she felt that she needed a degree. She wanted to go on for her Ph.D., but the biology department chair couldn't see giving up a slot for what he called "another bored faculty wife." Which is why she needed Mike to sponsor her.

Mike soon offered me a job washing glassware in the lab after school. He also invited our family to his farm in Pittsboro, about twenty miles south of Chapel Hill. I began to piece to-

17

gether Mike's backstory from things my mother told me, conversations around the lab, and his own stories—he told a lot of stories about himself. I thought he was the most interesting person I had ever met, and he seemed to share my opinion.

Mike's IQ was supposedly in the neighborhood of 180. Allegedly, he had never received less than the maximum score on any standardized test. He also had a photographic memory. I discovered this when I borrowed a Philip José Farmer novel from him. When I returned the book, Mike said, "Wasn't it great on the top of page 218 when he wrote..." and then spewed off several sentences of text. I turned to the top of page 218 and found the sentences Mike had just repeated verbatim.

Mike had played football at Brandeis but left early—supposedly because he spilled the beans about the quarterback being a ringer who had played pro ball in Canada. He had earned a bachelor's from Brooklyn College, studied law at NYU, acquired two master's degrees from the University of Indiana, and finally added a doctorate in molecular genetics from the University of Illinois. Then he was hired by UNC as an assistant professor.

At one point, Mike confided that he had left an educational institution early because he had been caught in a tryst with a dean's underage daughter. It took me a while to realize that he had been married when he left Brandeis, his first school. I didn't know what to make of this story.

Pictures of Mike as a graduate student showed an intriguing, slightly intimidating figure with a shaved head, goatee, and weight lifter's build. One photograph featured a huge, colorful parrot—a hyacinth macaw—perched on his shoulder. Around campus, he was almost as widely recognized as his Irish wolfhound, Lilly. Between classes Mike earned black belts in judo and kendo and zipped around on a BSA motorcycle. The bike had an irritating dead spot in the acceleration curve until a frustrated mechanic delivered a solid kick to the bike's magneto. After that, it was the fastest road racer in southern Indiana. Mike proved its worth in illegal competitions, then sold it for a bundle.

Mike and his wife Lea were not close. The first time I saw their bedroom, I noticed that someone had driven a fist into the door to the connecting bathroom. The bedroom was small and completely filled with a king-size bed. When I asked Mike about it, he said he wanted a bed in which he could sleep as far from his wife as possible. Mike also special-ordered a huge truck, a four-door F-350 long bed, without power steering because he wanted a truck his wife couldn't drive.

Mike's father's death gave him money to burn, and around the same time his wife moved back to New York. I have a hunch the inheritance made divorce possible. Mike went on a spree of buying tropical fish and guns, and he also started acquiring exotic animals for the farm. These included guanacos, wild ancestors of the llama, and rheas, large, flightless birds related to ostriches and emus. Then he drove down to Miami, where most of the nation's animal importers are situated, and came back with a tiger cub. In those days you could just buy one without any oversight. He named her Gretchen.

Gretchen grew quickly and was soon too big to be treated like a funny-looking dog, so Mike had a moat dug around a knoll with an old, decaying farmhouse. The land inside the trench gave Gretchen about an acre to call her own, the house provided shelter, and the moat supplied drinking water. The moat also ensured that she had no footing for jumping the twelve-foot fence. Once Mike had Gretchen situated, he went back to Miami. This time he came back with a jaguar cub.

19

In the spring of 1972, I began to hear unfamiliar sounds in our house—sobs and shouts from my parents' bedroom. In May, my parents called an impromptu family meeting. This was scary, because we had never had a family meeting before. My mother said she was moving out. "Each of you will have to choose which parent to live with," our parents informed us. I stayed in the house with my father and my older sister, Lianne. My two younger sisters went with my mom.

Several weeks after the split, I was washing dishes in the lab when Mike called me into his office. He sat me down and leaned back in his chair, hands clasped behind his head. "I just want you know," he said, "that I love your mother very much. I didn't want to fall in love with her, but I did. I also care about you very much, and I can promise you that I'd never do anything intentionally to hurt you."

This was way too much information for me to take in. It opened up possibilities I wasn't ready to think about, and I was embarrassed I had not seen it coming. I turned my head away and looked at the piranhas. By then there were two—different subspecies in adjacent tanks. The newer one, Fred, was chewing on a pork chop hung from a twisted coat hanger. I stared at them, thinking: This is not a man who plays by the rules.

My father had always worked a lot and wasn't around the house much when I was growing up. This didn't change after the split, and he was around even less when he found a new girlfriend. He sometimes had dinner with us, but he often just brought home groceries and then left again. Some days Lianne and I would have beer for breakfast and chocolate ice cream for dinner. I was fourteen, and Lianne was sixteen. A six-bedroom, three-bath house can feel awfully empty with two teenagers living in it.

The final straw came just before Christmas, when I found out that my father had planned a Christmas dinner at his girlfriend's. Lianne and I were invited, but it was the first Christmas since the split, and I was angry that he hadn't felt the need to do something special for the loyal remnants of his own family. By that time, my mother had moved in with Mike at the farm. I called her and told her I wanted to have Christmas dinner there. Somehow I just never went home.

You see, my father didn't play by the rules either, or he would have been there for Lianne and me. And, of course, neither did my mother, otherwise she wouldn't have had an affair. It seemed to me that there were no rules, and so I should do what served me best. I could lead a boring, neglected life in my father's house, or go live on a farm where I could play with big cats. It was, as they say, a no-brainer.

Or was it? It took me a long time to learn that there are rules, *if we choose them*. And if I had played by the rules back then, perhaps I wouldn't have left my sister all alone in the big, old, empty house.

21

Role Model

MIKE INSINUATED HIMSELF INTO my family long before my parents announced their separation. In addition to inviting us to the farm to play with Gretchen and ride horses, he bought gifts for us kids.

His first gift to me was an iguana. It was a small, inoffensive, sedentary lizard that ate fruits, vegetables, and an occasional mealworm.

Next he bought my sister Gwenn a squirrel monkey named Chico that ate bananas from our fingers and enjoyed being held. He also had a propensity to urinate while perched on someone's shoulder.

Seeing how much I enjoyed the iguana, Mike bought me a tegu lizard. This beast was almost three feet long, counting its tail, and a serious carnivore. Whenever I took it out for exercise, I had to summon all my nerve to pick it up when it was time to return the lizard to its cage. One day it escaped into Gwenn's room, and when I tried to grab it, it scrambled away, leaving me with a grip on its tail, which snapped off in my hand. The tegu immediately emptied the contents of its stomach—a partially digested mixture of raw egg and hamburger—onto Gwenn's carpet and bolted under the furniture. The bloody stump of a tail thrashed in my hand. As Chico howled, Gwenn yelled in fury, "Get that thing out of here!"

I spent more time at the farm after my parents' split and became increasingly attached to Arrow, the younger of Mike's two English mastiffs. I began to fantasize about adopting him as my own. I was in the hospital with an ankle bleed when my mother told me Arrow's toe had become infected. X-rays showed that a small piece of shot, a legacy from when Mike had broken up a mastiff fight with a shotgun blast to the ground, had lodged in the toe. Mike urged the vet to amputate, but the vet insisted he could save the toe. Arrow went into septic shock and died.

Mike had bought Gwenn a bichon frise named Truman, and with Arrow gone, Mike decided he would buy me my own dog. By that time, my mother had moved in with him. The plan was for the dog to live at the farm. I think Mike knew that my move to the farm was inevitable—or would be once I had a dog out there.

I had no idea what kind of dog I wanted, but I knew I didn't want a yapper like Truman, so I was devastated when Mike informed me, "Son, I'm afraid you'll have to get a small dog. Too many big dogs around this place already. Too many fights." A few days later, Mike handed me books on four breeds and suggested I choose one of them. It seemed I would be getting a bloodhound, a rottweiler, a Rhodesian ridgeback, or a bouvier des Flandres. In Mike's world, a small dog was anything less than 150 pounds. I chose a bouvier.

I was in the hospital again when my puppy arrived. Mike had said I would need to get a female, but at the last minute the breeder asked if we would we take a male, and Mike surprised me by saying yes. I had compiled a short list of goddess names from Teutonic mythology, but I had no male names picked out. During my hospital stay, I had been working my way through a science fiction series by Keith Laumer. The protagonist is James Retief, who violates the rules of intergalactic diplomacy as he pragmatically prevents interplanetary warfare. For lack of a better name, I called the puppy Retief, which was quickly shortened to Tief.

Mike and my mom met the plane and drove to Mike's office, which was down the street from the hospital. They put on white lab coats, put the puppy in a box, commandeered a wheelchair at one of the side entrances to the hospital, and snuck the puppy up to the pediatric ward in the freight elevator, hoping no one would notice the wimpering.

I was so excited to see the puppy that at first I didn't notice when a nurse walked in. "You can't have a dog in here," she screamed. "It's against the rules. How did you get in here? You have to take him away." We tried to convince her to turn a blind eye for a few more minutes but without success. "What if my supervisor finds out? I could be fired. Don't you know this is a hospital?"

I consider pointing out that the thirteen-pound bundle of fur in my bed belonged in the hospital. After all, he still had white bandages on his ears, which had been cropped, and his tail, which had been docked. But I sensed that any flip comment would send the nurse howling into the hall.

The day I came home from the hospital, I suffered a horrendous bout of diarrhea. Mike gave me strong muscle relaxants that made me nearly comatose and stuck me in a spare bedroom in the main house. He shut Tief in with me, and the puppy spent the entire night whining at the bedroom door, trying to squeeze his body through the one-inch gap at the bottom. I couldn't move, but I also couldn't sleep.

Tief was really sweet in some ways. If you were crying anywhere on the farm, he would find you and comfort you. He taught the other dogs to shit in the woods, not near the house. He put up with Truman's constant attempts to assert dominance, and once when Truman was swimming in the pond and started to tire, Tief swam out, put his nose under Truman's belly, and pushed the struggling dog to shore.

But he also loved to herd things.

Bouviers are cow herders, but the only cows we had were the downers donated as tiger food, so Tief herded whatever he could find. He preferred Volkswagens and horses. One day we had to rescue two people in a Beetle who were driving in circles around a neighbor's yard while Tief lunged at their tires. When there were no Beetles to chase, he would nip at the horses' heels until they kicked him with their hind legs. He always turned at the last minute and took the blow in the ribs with a thump audible a hundred yards away. Then he would fly backward several feet and roll across the grass. Newcomers to the farm reflexively ran to his aid, fearing for his life, but Tief simply gathered himself and went at it again.

The worst problem was Tief herding sheep into the farm pond, where the lambs drowned. We wanted to slow him down enough that his targets could escape, so we chained him to a cinder block. When he chased the sheep, the cinder block bounced across the field behind him.

It took us a while to perfect the technology, though. The first challenge was finding a strong enough collar. Tief had a tendency to "lose" collars by letting them settle on his shoulder and then shrugging until they snapped. We finally found a wide, thick, leather collar with a sturdy D-ring. The second challenge was finding the right chain. First we tried the kind of chain we used to tether goats and other animals. Tief would wedge the cinder block between two trees and lean until the chain snapped. We bought a tow chain, and that seemed to do the trick.

The perfect material for the third and final piece of the apparatus—the weight—eluded us. A cinder block was only marginally adequate. Tief figured out that he could run full-tilt through a cluster of boulders, bouncing the cinder block over the rocks until—crack!—no more cinder block. Fortunately, we had plenty of cinder blocks—enough to last until Tief outgrew his puppy exuberance.

Even as an adult, though, Tief's enthusiasm sometimes got the better of him. I blame myself. For one thing, I had named him. It turns out *retief* is an obsolete French adjective that translates as stubborn, unruly, unmanageable, and balky. He was just living up to his name.

For another thing, Tief was exactly the dog I needed him to be. He was always true to his nature. He was never deterred by obstacles or the burdens he dragged behind him. He never held back and never backed down. He was fiercely protective of those he loved and refused to be left out. He embodied the kind of will I would need to survive both my hemophilia and the challenges I would face on the farm and later in life.

We were made for each other. Tief wasn't just my dog—he was also my role model.

The Monkey Died

ON THE FIRST WARM NIGHT of the year, I fell asleep with my bedroom window open. In the middle of the night, I woke to find a jaguar at the foot of my bed.

I looked down at my legs. The jaguar had gnawed a foot-wide hole through the bedspread, centered roughly above my left ankle. He appeared to have been working on the sheet, which was soaked with drool. With a roguish smile, he let me know, playfully: I could have had your legs. Then he yawned, exposing two-inch canines in an artfully contrived gesture of disinterest, and bounded out. I closed the window and went back to sleep.

The jaguar was named Gregor, after the Austrian botanist Gregor Mendel. He was my stepfather's second big cat (after the tiger Gretchen). Mike's menagerie was expanding quickly, but outside of Tief, Gregor was my favorite critter.

Gregor lived in the house for several months, but when he broke an expensive antique vase, Mike banished him by chaining him to a large oak between the main house and my trailer. The chain reached my bedroom window. It also reached the

27

ramp that led to the front door, and it became nearly impossible to enter the house from the front without being hunted. Gregor's idea of a good time was to wrap himself around the legs of anyone carrying an armload of groceries. When Gregor had no humans to hunt, he stalked the African pygmy goats that ran loose in the yard.

Gregor was maybe a year old when Mike bought another jaguar, a female he named Frossie. The plan was for her to become Gregor's mate, but Mike didn't have a cage for either one. Mike had had a chain-link cage built, which in the long term he intended to use for the jaguars, but when Frossie arrived, it was home to Margo, a black gibbon, and Jeff, an Asiatic black bear. Mike had expected that the animals would live completely apart, as if the cage was a two-story condo—the gibbon in the air and the bear on the ground—but Margo adopted Jeff as a pet. Periodically, she would settle down next to the bear and try to groom him.

To socialize the two jaguars, Mike gave Frossie a chain of her own, close to Gregor's. Their world became a Venn diagram, and in the overlap of their two circles, they played constantly. They were very affectionate together. One night we went out to a movie and came back to find Frossie lying still on the ground with Gregor's chain wrapped around her neck. We unwrapped the chain, and my mother and I tried to resuscitate Frossie. Gregor watched solemnly, mournfully, as we pounded on her chest and one of us—perhaps it was me, perhaps it was my mother—held her mouth shut and blew air into her nose. It was no use.

It is hard to explain why Mike had so many exotic animals. Sometimes I tell people that he thought he was Tarzan. That isn't true, of course, but it is as close to the truth as just about anything else I could say. The bottom line, though, was that he really loved animals. He loved them as much as anyone I have ever met. But loving someone or something isn't the same as being a good caretaker. With so many animals around, it was inevitable that I would witness a lot of death. Most animals at the tiger farm lived long, healthy lives and were probably better off than most captive wild animals (although I don't know if that is saying a lot).

Sometimes Mike would take astounding steps to save an animal, like the time his wolfhound, Darwin, was temporarily paralyzed. The vet recommended putting him down, but Mike made a sling that he hung from the ceiling, and he took care of Darwin and cleaned up after him until he could walk again.

Gregor remained a sweet, affectionate creature, and he lived for many more years. He died while attempting to mate with another jaguar, one with a nasty disposition—she put a canine through the top of his skull. Violent aggression during breeding isn't unusual for jaguars. They're very human that way.

But some of the deaths were hard for me to accept, like the ball python Mike gave me as a gift. Of all the reptiles I owned, this was the one I liked most. But it refused to eat. Mike insisted that force-feeding it was the solution. He grabbed the python by the neck and forced its jaw open, then he inserted a cube of beef and pushed it down the snake's gullet with his fingers. The rest of the snake thrashed wildly in the air, churning like the agitator on a washing machine. Mike repeated this act three times, maybe four, until we noticed that the snake was limp. "Shit, piss, and corruption," said Mike, uttering his favorite string of expletives. I didn't know who to blame more, Mike for force-feeding the python so brutally, or me for allowing it.

Once we took in a horribly matted stray Persian. We tried to comb out the knots in her coat, but it was impossible. "Give her to me," Mike said one evening. "And someone bring me the good scissors." When he had her on his lap, he pinned her with his arms and thighs and began to cut. She struggled against his grip, howling, but he kept working. He had removed most of the knots before we noticed the openings, the places where he had cut not just hair, but also skin. There were holes in her flesh the size of quarters, and below only muscle showed.

"Don't worry," Mike said flatly. "We'll just take her in tomorrow and get her stitched up."

He also let two squirrel monkeys, Chico and Paco, loose in the yard. They were so cute racing through the trees. In the morning they would clamor for pieces of banana. They would also drop down onto the backs of the pygmy goats like little jockeys, grab their mounts' horns, and steer them by pulling on one horn and pushing on the other.

The monkeys would sneak into the aviary and steal food from the parrots and the toucan. Then Mike picked up a pair of caracals, tuft-eared lynxes from north Africa. They are great leapers and can pluck birds from the air. Mike converted the aviary into a caracal cage, only nobody warned the squirrel monkeys. Slowed by the winter cold and unfamiliar with caracals, one became dinner. We suspect that the other one simply froze to death.

One of the first stories Mike shared with me was about a fire at his parents' Brooklyn home. When the smoke cleared, firefighters entered the brownstone to look for the source of the fire and to check for hot spots. The first man into the basement ran back up the stairs, yelling about alligators and giant snakes. His buddies scoffed. The next firefighter down stayed just long enough to confirm the first man's account.

Even as a kid Mike collected animals, but at some point his parents said he couldn't get any more. This presented Mike with two problems: how to afford new animals and where to keep them. The first problem he solved by collecting local creatures and trading them to area zoos for more exotic surplus animals, typically snakes and lizards. The second problem was also solvable. He decided to keep his growing menagerie in the basement, where his father, an attorney, stored his old legal files.

Mike somehow talked a zoo out of a baby monkey, which he swaddled and placed in the open drawer of a file cabinet. When he went out, he left a lamp shining on the infant to make sure it didn't catch a chill. The monkey apparently began to explore and knocked over the lamp, which set the papers on fire.

As I got to know Mike, I came to see this as the quintessential Michael Bleyman story. It features the amusing antics of a resourceful rogue who truly loved animals, a charming rascal always working the angle while straddling or even crossing the line. You couldn't help but love a kid like that, or the man he would become.

But in the end, the monkey died.

Jason and the Hells Angels

WHEN I FIRST MET MIKE, he had a foster daughter named Diane. As a teenager, she was too much for her parents to handle. Mike had a way with wild things, so he took her in. She left the farm about the time I arrived, taking Moses, her Neapolitan mastiff. After that, she got a second dog, a young Irish wolfhound she named Jason.

One evening, Diane showed up unexpectedly. She was crying and panicky. The night before, her mastiff had suddenly started bleeding from his rectum and had died. She found a note that read, "We got your dog. We'll be back tomorrow for the other one."

"They must have fed him ground glass," said Diane. She was certain that whoever killed Moses planned to do something similar to Jason, the wolfhound puppy. She told us she had been living with a member of the Hells Angels Motorcycle Club and had left her "old man" without his blessing. Knowing a little about Diane's past, I suspected there was more to the story, but clearly she had pissed off some badass biker and was afraid for herself as well as for Jason.

We sat around the table—my mother, Mike, Diane, and I—and discussed options. One possibility was for someone to go home with Diane and stay up all night to keep watch—and to fight off the Hells Angels if they showed up.

I volunteered, even though I was only sixteen, was about five foot three, weighed at most 115 pounds, and had never been up all night. Nor, for that matter, had I ever been in a gunfight or a serious fight of any kind. Plus, as a hemophiliac, I don't take particularly well to gunshot wounds. But I had gotten to that point in my life only by ignoring limitations. I had always insisted I could do anything, no matter what anyone else might say. When my parents told me I couldn't have a bike without training wheels, for example, I borrowed a teenage neighbor's six-speed and taught myself to ride, even though I couldn't reach the seat.

So while Mike, Diane, and my mother continued talking, I went into the master bedroom, unlocked the gun cabinet, and started arming myself. As a novice, I had no idea what kind of weapons I would need. Would I be shooting to warn, to wound, or to kill? Would the fighting be close in, or would I need a weapon with range? Would there be one biker or many? Since I had no answers, I prepared for any possibility.

I strapped on two shoulder holsters. Under the left arm, I shoved Mike's untraceable Colt .45, and under the right, a 9 mm Browning. I also belted a tiny, .25-caliber automatic to one leg. I chose an over-under as my main gun. The top barrel fired a .22 long-shot rifle round, and the bottom fired a .410 shotgun shell. My hope was that I would not need anything too lethal. Still, I thought, I might require something more, in case things got nasty. In case I needed to kill someone.

I was trying to decide between the Winchester Model 12 shotgun (it was a 12-gauge pump action; I thought the double-barreled 10-gauge would be overkill, plus firing it always bruised my shoulder) and the Weatherby .300 big-game rifle when my mother came in.

"We have decided to send Huxley instead," she said, referring to one of Mike's dogs, an English mastiff that weighed more than 200 pounds. "He is trained to never take food from strangers." She pointed out that I had a math test the next day. "You need to study," she said, as if this was the deciding factor.

I unloaded the weapons and stripped off the shoulder holsters. I was both relieved and disappointed. If I had gone to fight the Hells Angels, I might have gotten out of my test.

I told this story once to someone who responded, "It is a story about something that didn't happen." And to an extent that's true. I didn't end up in a gun battle. But it is also a story about something that did happen. It is one of those "What the hell were the parents thinking?" stories, but it is also a story about a sixteen-year-old thinking it was appropriate to gear up like that.

To understand why, I have to tell another story, one about my time in the basement.

In the summer before sixth grade, my family moved into a house with a partially finished basement. I had a lot of ankle bleeds in those days. When the pain got so bad I couldn't sleep, I spent my nights down there, watching television. We didn't have 24/7 television then, and when the last station went off the air, usually around midnight, there was a brief image of a waving flag while the national anthem played, and then there was nothing but a cross-like test pattern. Staring at that pattern for hours on end, I would swear to god, any god, that I would believe, I would pray, I would serve, if only he—or she—would take the pain away. It never worked; I never did find religion.

Many nights, I didn't fall asleep until sunrise. I asked myself a lot of questions during those long vigils. By this time, I had stopped asking, pointlessly, Why me? Instead, I played out various scenarios in my head. In one, I was in a life raft with several other people, but the raft would not stay afloat with all of us in it, and there wasn't enough food and water to go around. Someone would have to go overboard into the frigid sea, where sharks were circling. I asked myself if I could be the one to jump, whether I would have that kind of strength. Yes, was the answer that came back to me over and over. Always, Yes.

I asked other, similar questions. For example, could I jump off a cliff if it would save lives? Again the answer was yes. Meanwhile, my family slept soundly upstairs because I had taken it upon myself to jump into the basement where sharks shredded my ankles and I refused to cry out, afraid I might wake everyone.

Amid all these questions, there was one I never asked: Are these the kinds of questions a ten-year-old should be dealing with? But they were exactly the questions a boy might ask if he was ashamed and needed to justify being here.

You see, I didn't feel I deserved to stay in the life raft, not unless there was room for everyone else. After all, I was defective. I had been born broken. How could I supplant someone who had a full life to look forward to, someone whole and normal? The best possible resolution to my situation, it seemed, would be to die a noble death. I didn't think about suicide—that would have seemed cowardly and pointless—but I did think about making the ultimate sacrifice. It would offer redemption, wash away my shame, validate my existence.

These scenarios were my way of self-calibrating, my own personal test patterns.

That night when Diane came over to tell us that Moses was dead and to ask for our help, I had been briefly offered the possibility of living out the kind of scenario I obsessed over all those nights in the basement: dying in a hail of bullets to protect a woman and her puppy.

Lolita the Chimp

MAINTAINING MIKE'S MENAGERIE required frequent trips, and I often went along. One of his regular stops was Cooke's Buffalo Ranch in Concord, North Carolina. Cooke's was a Western store. Old Man Cooke had a herd of bison in his pasture, and for a few bucks you could ride past them on a replica stagecoach. He also had a small roadside zoo. On one visit we discovered the zoo had a new attraction, a chimpanzee named Lolita. (I try not to think too hard about why someone would name a chimp Lolita.)

I thought I knew what chimps looked like, but what I had seen were a few movies and television shows. I didn't realize that the trained chimpanzees were cuddly little juveniles. Lolita, on the other hand, was a young adult. She had a black face and a mouth full of very large teeth that she displayed by curling back her lips. When she stood fully erect, she was taller than me. What struck me most was the power of her forearms, which seemed twice the length of mine, with thick cords of muscle. I knew that if I got too close, she could grab me, dismember me, and pull my body parts through the bars.

Lolita's cage was a former drunk tank. The county had recently built a new jail, and Cooke had purchased the old drunk tank. It was a freestanding iron cell, a cube roughly six feet wide on the sides but slightly taller, perhaps eight feet, in height. A tow chain circled her neck and was held in place with a padlock. The chain had chafed away some of her hair.

It seemed a horrible way to live, but part of me was thankful for the bars. Then Old Man Cooke did something strange: He walked closer to the cage and stuck out his foot. Lolita reached through and daintily untied his shoelaces. Then she tied them up again. Untie, tie, untie, tie, untie, tie. Cooke told us she would do this as long as he kept his foot next to her cage. I looked at the cage, I looked at the chain, I looked into her dark brown eyes. Seeing no hostility and a great deal of sadness, what else could I do? I offered her my sneaker.

A few weeks later, Mike informed us he had purchased Lolita. Tim, one of Mike's many weekend volunteers, had agreed to help move her. Mike also made it clear that he was counting on my assistance, though there wasn't much I could offer. Tim arrived on moving day on his Harley Hog. When we climbed into the cab of the F-350, Tim brought his motorcycle helmet with him. "Protection," he said, pounding on it smugly.

At Cooke's, we tied Lolita to a post while Mike, Tim, and some of Cooke's workers loaded the tank into the bed of the truck. Mike decided it was too chilly to transport Lolita inside her cage, and his solution was to put her in the cab with us. It was a four-door cab with two bench seats. He passed the free end of the chain through the split rear window and anchored it to the side of the truck bed. The chain kept Lolita from climbing into the front seat. It did nothing, however, to prevent her from reaching across the seat and snapping me in half.

For the first part of the drive, Lolita occupied herself with dismantling the truck. She pulled out the dome light, unscrewed the door locks, and managed to yank loose one of the window cranks. Because her fidgeting made him nervous, Tim put on his helmet—and as soon as he did: Wham! Wham! Wham! Lolita repeatedly and forcefully whacked the back of Tim's head. He sat there for the better part of an hour, absorbing blow after blow. The whole time, I tried to make myself invisible. Tim was a body builder. He was over six feet tall and probably weighed about 250 pounds—and he had a helmet. At that time, I probably weighed 115 pounds and had not yet reached my full stature of five foot six. I was a little guy with a skinny neck and no helmet. I recalled all the stories I had ever heard about hemophiliacs dying from cranial hemorrhaging. If Lolita started flailing on my head, I thought, surely I am dead.

Somehow, though, we survived. Mike and Tim unloaded the drunk tank in the middle of the yard and led Lolita into it. "Man," said Tim as he was leaving, "I'm sure glad I brought my helmet."

Later, we learned more about Lolita's history. It seemed a man had trained a young chimpanzee to ride on the back of his motorcycle. He had wrecked the bike and killed the chimp, so he had bought Lolita as a replacement. Lolita had been too old to train and hated riding on the motorcycle, absolutely hated it. The man had given up and sold her to Cooke. Lolita wasn't hitting Tim so much as his helmet. If he hadn't put it on, she would have left him alone. And I was never at risk.

Mike had no other place to keep Lolita, so he left her in the drunk tank. From time to time, he would take her out so she could exercise and he could clean her cage. He would lead her from the tank by the chain and tie her to one of the trees in the yard. One day, when he decided to put her back in her cage, she wasn't ready to go. Mike insisted by yanking the chain, and she responded by biting him on the hand, practically severing his thumb. Mike didn't miss a beat. With his intact hand, he picked up a beef bone the dogs had left in the yard and slammed it down on her head. I half expected to see her topple over, but instead she staggered momentarily and then raced contritely back into the tank. Mike shut the door, ran inside to grab a towel to wrap his hand in, and got my mom to drive him to the hospital.

Even after she bit Mike, I spent time with Lolita, often offering my shoe or feeding her fruit through the bars. But when I think back on her time with us, I am struck by how much I feared her. It is what most people would expect, I think. But fear wasn't really in my vocabulary. As a child with hemophilia, someone who could easily die by falling off a bicycle or mistiming a leap from the diving board, I never would have gone anywhere or done anything if I had grown up in fear. At the farm, it wasn't good to show fear, especially when I was going into a tiger's cage on crutches or waking to find a jaguar at the foot of my bed. It wasn't that I was never afraid, but I rarely acknowledged my fear even to myself.

I think I feared Lolita because if I had been her, I would have attacked, and that's why it always felt like an attack was imminent. After all, her previous owner terrorized her. Cooke put her in chains and imprisoned her, and Mike kept her under the same conditions. To his credit, Mike eventually sold Lolita to a zoo, and I wondered if that was his plan all along, to get her away from Cooke and into a bigger place where she would have her own kind for company. But I don't know that for sure, and she couldn't have known it either.

40

Tim triggered her PTSD when he put on his helmet. Mike led her around by a chain and slammed a bone down on her skull when she demanded more freedom. And me? Could I claim innocence because I was just along for the ride?

Fear is a complex emotion. Sometimes it is simply about self-preservation, but I think it can also be a secondary emotion. Like anger, it can mask something deeper. Perhaps in my case, that something was guilt.

I don't think I openly feared Lolita because she was more deadly than the other animals I lived with, or because she was at heart a wild and uncontrollable beast. I think I feared her because she was so damn human.

Be Like Mike

WE WERE ON OUR WAY TO ATLANTA one rainy night, driving along a stretch of Interstate 85 through South Carolina, and a tractor-trailer truck pulled over when Mike tried to pass. "Shit, piss, and corruption," said Mike the first time. But when it happened again, he exploded.

"He's playing games. That fucker's playing games. I'll show him. Give me my gun."

I knew he was talking to me. Mike almost always traveled with a gun, although he did not have a concealed-weapons permit. Usually he carried a .25-caliber automatic in his briefcase. I was seated on the forward bench seat of our Econoline van, just behind the driver's seat, and the briefcase was on the floor at my feet.

"What the hell are you going to do?" asked my mom.

"I'm going to shoot out his fucking tire, that's what!"

The first time I shot a gun, it was Mike's .22-caliber target rifle. This was during one of the early visits to the farm, before the family fell apart. Mike attached paper targets to a stretch of field fencing with clothespins, and my sisters and I squeezed off shots from the bed of his battered red Toyota pickup. At the time, Gretchen the tiger was a cub. She had the run of the place and spent most of her time stalking people for fun. When my sister Gwenn's turn to shoot came, she concentrated so hard that she forgot about the tiger. Gretchen closed on the truck with a sudden burst, pounced, easily cleared the side of the bed, and landed squarely on Gwenn's back.

Gwenn huffed. "Gretchen, get off," she said, and calmly pulled the trigger.

The first time I shot a handgun, it was Mike's .357 magnum. Mike had handed me the huge Colt revolver with no instructions. I raised it in the air and pointed the barrel upward as I cocked it, emulating Clint Eastwood's nameless character in spaghetti Westerns. My finger was on the trigger as I did this, and the gun fired immediately. The muzzle blast blew my bangs off my forehead, and the round missed my skull by no more than a couple inches.

The first rifle of my own was a present for earning Eagle Scout rank at fourteen. By this time, my mother had moved out, and Mike and she were dating openly. After the Court of Honor ceremony, my mother led me out to her Pinto. She opened the back and threw aside a wool blanket. Under the blanket was a World War I-vintage Swiss rifle, a straight-action Schmidt-Ruben.

My oldest sister Lianne, who was standing behind me, began to cry. "Guns are for killing," she screamed. "You're making my little brother into a killer."

My mother lashed back. "Hunting was the only thing that kept meat on our table during the war."

This gun, however, was never intended for game. Nearly as long as I was tall, it was so heavy I could barely lift it, and it took a unique and hard-to-find shell. But I thought it looked nice on my bedroom wall.

For my fifteenth birthday, Mike and my mother took me to a gun shop, where I picked out a Ruger 10/22, a .22-caliber rifle suitable for target practice and squirrel hunting. When I brought the gun home, I went to my room and practiced loading it. While I was examining how the safety worked, I inadvertently fired the gun. The bullet ricocheted off my metal wastebasket and buried itself in the wall. Fortunately, I always kept spackling compound and paint handy for such occasions. After filling the bullet hole and painting it, I tried with limited success to straighten out the wastebasket before I went downstairs, where my mother was visiting with my sisters. When my mother asked about the noise, I told her, "I tripped and fell on my wastebasket."

Later, I bought a Ruger single-action, .45-caliber revolver with my own money. I also had my grandfather's classic Winchester Model 12 shotgun re-blued and had the stock cut down and fitted with a recoil pad so it wouldn't bruise my shoulder.

In the first year that I knew Mike, I had gone from never being around guns to having four of my own.

Then came what I think of as the rage years, after Mike was denied tenure, lost his job, and according to my mother, started abusing prescription meds. Mike became a dangerous man. He once threatened to beat a man with a shovel because the man started to fill his car with gas when it was Mike's turn at the pump. So the road rage incident on the way to Atlanta wasn't a complete surprise.

I doubted Mike could hit the truck's tires at seventy miles per hour, at night, in the driving rain, and if he did, I seriously doubted that such a small gun would make much of a difference to a semi. The back end of the trailer rode on eight huge tires. Even if Mike managed to shoot out one, the truck would keep going. Still, I had no doubt that if he did hit it, and if hitting it did make a difference and the truck suddenly fishtailed, careened, jackknifed, or flipped right in front of us, then we would all be dead.

Ignoring my mother, Mike yelled over his shoulder at me, "Give me the god damn gun."

I lied. "I don't know where it is."

"It's in the briefcase."

"Mike, don't," said my mother.

"Where's the briefcase?" I asked.

"You are not going to shoot that truck!" my mother insisted.

Again he ignored her. "It's back there, under your seat."

"I got it," I said, meaning the briefcase. The automatic was lying right on top in its suede clip-on holster.

"Good, now give me the gun."

"I can't find it."

"Give me the god damn gun!"

"I don't see it."

"Don't lie to me, son."

"I'm looking."

"Give me the fucking gun!"

I was afraid to stall any longer and picked up the gun to hand it to him, but just at that moment Mike managed to get past the truck.

Around the same time, Mike and my mother started fighting a lot. A couple of times it got so loud and vicious that I snuck into their bedroom and unloaded all the guns. This worried me because I could only imagine what would happen if one of the big cats got out and Mike went after it with an empty

45

gun. So I snuck back in and reloaded everything as soon as they calmed down.

Then there was the time a dog went missing. It was Sal, a long-haired dachshund that showed up one day and stuck around. We eventually found his body on the side of the road, and to me it seemed clear that he had been hit by a car, but Mike saw a hole in Sal's skin and became convinced a neighbor had shot the dog. His answer was to pull a cow haunch out of the freezer and set it down near the road. Then he had me get every gun we owned, and together we emptied them all into that haunch. It must have been a half-hour, nonstop volley. I hadn't had time to find earplugs, and my ears rang for hours. "There," said Mike when we ran out of ammo. And then, as if every neighbor in the hamlet of Hanks Chapel had had a ringside seat. "They won't mess with us again."

When I went off to college later that year, I divested myself of all my guns. I left the shotgun with my mother and eventually returned it to my grandfather's family in Pennsylvania. Mike bought the handgun from me. I am not sure what happened to the .22, and I am pretty sure that the Schmidt-Ruben, which had no resale value, remained at the farm.

Before I met Mike, my life was boring, and my father was pretty much absent. I had no identity other than that of a hemophiliac. Mike, however, was a constant, larger-than-life presence, so I had styled myself after him. I did the things he did, like collecting fish, smoking cigars, and going to Bruce Lee movies. Guns were a way of relating to Mike, but they were also part of creating a bigger, bolder, more distinctive, and more manly me. Sort of a mini-Mike.

I liked guns because I wanted to be like Mike. But after seeing him when he was angry and violent and high, the guns

46

stopped being amusing toys and badges of manly eccentricity. They played such a big part in who he became, at least for a while, that I will never own a gun again.

Because now I don't want to be like Mike at all—certainly not that Mike, anyway.

Jeff the Bear

IN MY TWENTIES, I WORKED at a balloon company. I delivered bouquets, built balloon sculptures for parties, and worked in the shop as a cashier. The shop sold party supplies and stuffed animals. A few days before Thanksgiving one year, a very tall man in a raincoat walked in, looked around, and then left. As soon as he walked out the door, I noticed that a stuffed animal, a turkey, was missing. I bolted out the door, picked out the man in the crowd, and followed him for several blocks, slowly working my way closer. I caught up to him while he was waiting for a walk signal and grabbed the turkey out of his hand.

He just looked down at me sadly and said, "I'm sorry. It's my little boy's birthday, and I don't have money for a present." At that moment, I wished I'd never followed him. I silently took the turkey and returned to the store. My boss, who was also a good friend, was furious. "You could have gotten killed over a stuffed animal," he yelled. "Why would you do that?"

I knew why, but I also knew that I couldn't explain it. It was because of Jeff the bear, Jason the Irish wolfhound, and of course, my stepfather, Mike.

During one of our family trips to buy exotic animals, Mike had picked up a tiny black bear cub that seemed too young to have been brought into the country legally. We speculated that a hunter had shot his mother and sold the cub on the black market. Mike asked one of the workers what kind of bear it was. "Himalayan bear," answered the worker. But Mike was confused by the man's heavy Cuban accent and heard, "He Malayan bear." So Mike believed he was buying a Malayan sun bear, rather than a Himalayan black bear, or moon bear.

We named the little guy after my Uncle Jeff, who was somewhat ursine in appearance, and he imprinted on Mike as if Mike was his long-lost mother. Jeff lived in a large crate at first but was allowed to accompany us around the farm without a leash.

The first time Jeff saw Mike enter the tiger compound, the cub flew into a rage. He charged the chain-link fence and began to scale it, howling. He seemed convinced that Mike needed his protection. Mike raced out of the cage and pulled Jeff off the fence. We found out later that Asiatic black bears sometimes tangle with tigers in the wild—and sometimes win.

Jeff's efforts to defend Mike from Gretchen made me wonder if I could ever do what Jeff had tried to do. Could I be as brave as that little bear? If Mike, or my mother for that matter, was under attack by one of the tigers, say, or a jaguar, would I rush into the cage to attempt a rescue?

Because I had been the boy in the basement, because I felt I needed to justify my existence by making a heroic sacrifice, surely I could enter an animal's cage to rescue a member of my family. After seeing that bear's courage, I had my doubts.

One afternoon we got a call from a boarding kennel. The owner wondered if we knew a woman named Diane who had a young wolfhound named Jason. Diane, it seemed, had checked Jason into the kennel and never returned to pick him up. Would we be willing to pay the bill and take the dog? the owner asked. Mike drove out to the kennel immediately.

Jason had a playful, affectionate disposition. At first we couldn't imagine how Diane could have abandoned such a sweet dog, but after a few phone calls, Mike pieced together some of the story. Diane had been working in a massage parlor, this much we had known, although she had insisted that she didn't work topless and didn't do "manual relief." We also knew she had been living with another member of the Hells Angels. Massage parlors in North Carolina were controlled largely by organized crime, but that hadn't stopped Diane from raiding the till when she found out the state police had issued a warrant for her arrest. She also stopped by her boyfriend's house long enough to steal his stereo. Then she had run for the Virginia state line. With the state police, organized crime, and the Hells Angels looking for her, it didn't seem likely she would be coming back for her dog anytime soon.

Mike quickly became attached to the puppy, and the puppy to him. Jason accompanied Mike everywhere, bounding up to greet him when he came out of the house each morning. Mike had a habit of fixing his breakfast to go and carrying it with him on his rounds. One morning, I emerged from the house and witnessed a happy sight—Mike, turkey drumstick dangling at his side, Jason prancing beside him. Then Jason grabbed the drumstick, and Mike reacted swiftly, yanking back his breakfast and delivering a solid kick to Jason's rib cage. Jason didn't make a sound, didn't take another step, didn't even stagger. He just fell over right where he was. Black-belted, steel-toed Mike had struck right above Jason's heart, which went into immediate arrest. Mike checked Jason's eyes, felt for a pulse, and tried to detect any sign of breathing. Then he stood up, shook his head, and walked away. The drumstick lay discarded in the dirt.

I went looking for Mike several minutes later and found him sitting behind one of the barns. He was sobbing pitifully, and I realized I had never seen him cry before. I turned and walked away, leaving him to his grief. He showed up about twenty minutes later to load the body in the back of the truck and bury it in the back pasture. "You know," he told me when he returned, "I really loved that dog."

Which brings me to a hot, late-summer day just before I left for college. The house was filled with the sound of fans, and the white noise muffled almost everything but not the horrible shouting. I needed to get outside, but the path from my bedroom to the front door took me past the room where my mother and Mike were fighting. As I walked by, I was careful to avoid looking at them, but out of the corner of my eye I saw Mike raise his fist as if to strike. Then he saw me.

"Keep on moving, son," he said, "if you know what's good for you."

I did exactly what I was told. I went outside. I kept thinking I should go back and confront him, rescue my mother. This was the test I had long feared, but the setting was my home, not one of the cages, and the angry, dangerous beast was not feline. This was my test, and I was failing it. I did not have Jeff's courage.

Instead of going back inside, I walked around the yard and tried to convince myself that I couldn't possibly have seen what I thought I saw. Slowly, I started to win myself over. The light was pretty bad. What I saw was only a blur in my peripheral vision. My mother didn't cry out or ask for help. I never saw him actually land a blow. Maybe my walking by was enough to change the outcome, I told myself. Maybe I really did save my mother.

Besides, even if it was true, even if I saw what I thought I saw, even if he did hit her, there was the memory of Jason. Mike loved that dog, and yet he struck out in anger and killed it. Mike loved me, but I have little doubt that if I had gone back in the house, I might have become another Jason.

Yet the truth of what happened weighed on me, and I tried to convince myself that if something like that came up again, I wouldn't walk away. Not even if it was something trivial—as trivial, say, as a stuffed turkey.

No Longer a Virgin

WHEN I ARRIVED AT COLLEGE IN 1975, one of my first tasks was to get laid. My plan was to stand out as an interesting character. I was counting on my car (a battered 1965 Mustang notchback with a 297 V-8), my dog, my snakes (a couple of endangered rosy boas), and the fact that I lived on an animal farm stocked with tigers and other exotic creatures.

I was unloading in the dorm parking lot, however, when another student pulled up in a flawless 1967 Camaro SS with a 396 in the engine compartment and a Bernese mountain dog in the back seat. And the Camaro was a convertible. By the end of the day, I discovered that my dog was one of three bouviers on campus. He wasn't even the only one in my dorm.

I was outclassed in the car department and easily matched in the dog department, and because the Mustang didn't have air conditioning, my snakes had died from the heat in my ride up. I figured I would have to fall back on a somewhat hokey Southern drawl and my trump card, the tiger tales, which would have to be played strategically because many people wouldn't believe me.

I met Julie my second week. She snuggled up to me during a party in my dorm suite. I wrapped my arms around her, and she invited me back to her room. I didn't even have to say anything about the tigers.

We did not fall asleep until midmorning. She told me about her boyfriend in high school, how they had been sexual for more than a year, how she thought they were broken up but neither of them was quite sure. Disentangling was proving to be difficult.

I told her about my high school sexual encounters—the school camping trip where a classmate invited me to share her sleeping bag, my time out behind the school with a candy striper I met in the hospital, and the senior class picnic where the bus was held up while teachers scoured the woods for two missing students. I implied that each of these encounters had led to intercourse.

The sad truth is, I lied—to her and, in a sense, to myself.

For the record, then, here is the truth. I was invited to share a sleeping bag with a classmate on a school overnight trip. I crawled in with her, pressed myself against her back, and slid my hands up to her breasts.

"No, no, no," she said. "Get out. Get out right now." And so I did.

"That was just too fast," she said. "If you'd taken your time, you could have stayed. It would have been nice."

"We could try again, more slowly this time."

"No," she said, "it's too late."

I met the candy striper when I was laid up in the hospital the summer before my senior year. She told me she would be attending my high school in the fall. When she told me her schedule, I realized I would be the teaching assistant in her

54

biology class. I told her the teacher had talked to me about helping with the section on human sexuality, and she said it would be great to learn about sexuality from me. "I am sure you would be a very good teacher," she said with a coy smile.

When school started, we took a walk on the trail down through the woods behind the school. We talked, we sat, she briefly allowed me to open her shirt and kiss her breasts. Walking back, she took my hand in hers. I grew self-conscious when we passed some classmates on the tennis courts and yanked my hand away. We made plans to get together in the cafeteria the next day, but when I saw her, I pulled her aside and told her, "I can't do this. I don't know how to do this. It's not about you. I'm just not ready."

It happened to be the truth. I had no models for relationships that I could trust, nothing I wanted to emulate in my own life—not my mother's and father's seemingly passionless and doomed marriage, and certainly not either of my parents' passionate but severely flawed second marriages.

She quickly found another boyfriend who wasn't so awkward, and for the rest of my senior year I watched them, wondering what it was like to be part of a couple, to have a girlfriend who liked you and wanted to express her affections. I had no way to explain to her that I wasn't ashamed of her; I was ashamed of myself.

In the woods at the senior picnic, the same woman who years earlier had invited me into her sleeping bag was no longer as interested in going slow. She allowed me to open her shirt and pull her bra aside, but even with things moving fast, there was no time for anything more. The bus was leaving, and teachers had been sent to look for us.

And this was the sum total of my sexual experience when Julie took me into her bed. So why the lies?

When I was in junior high, the neighborhood boys started poking around an empty house. The late owner, an elderly woman, had been a hoarder, and looking through the boxes in her garage provided hours of amusement. The house was an imposing brick structure that seemed out of place on a street of more modest homes. When I peered through the French doors that lined the wraparound porch, I discovered that the brick structure was a roofless façade. Inside I could see another house, a humble wooden home. One of the older kids told me the story of the encased house. Chapel Hill had banned the keeping of chickens inside city limits. The owner insisted on keeping her chickens, so she built the brick shell around her existing house. She kept her chickens in the courtyard between the two houses and could legally claim that her fowl were indoor pets.

As a young boy with hemophilia, I had done the same thing. I had built an edifice to hide the house within, to encase the broken boy, the bullied boy, the boy in pain. If I could not be fast or strong, I would be intelligent and highly capable. Brick by brick over the years I had built this outer shell, this other self I could present to the world, and I would do almost anything to preserve the illusion.

The earliest offense I remember came in third grade. Every time I changed schools, there was a petite blond girl who was better than me academically. I could always pick her out on my first day. In third grade, math was self-paced, and the teacher put a chart up on the wall where we could mark off our progress. It became clear toward the end of the year that the blond girl would finish ahead of me. So I cheated. I put Xs in boxes for assignments I hadn't done until I was ahead of her. Coming in second didn't fit with the construct, the ego-ideal, the persona of the supremely competent kid I was building.

It was the same way with sex. I was ill-prepared and wary when it came to sex and relationships, but being sexually inexperienced, much less a virgin—being anything but a worldly and competent lover—was inconsistent with my ego-ideal, and so I created a false sexual history and refused to acknowledge to Julie that my night with her was, in fact, my first time. It wasn't just that I lied to her; I believed so much in the edifice I had built that I inhabited my false story more fully than I inhabited my own truth. At some deep level, I believed the lies I told. And so I deprived myself of a possibly profound and tender moment. I cheated myself out of the only opportunity I will ever have to experience losing my virginity.

Home Again

SHORTLY AFTER I LEFT FOR COLLEGE, Mike went off on one of his animal trips. When he returned, he left it to my mother to clean out the van. And when she did, she found a blanket belonging to Anita, one of Mike's former students. "What the hell was he thinking?" my mother asked me. "Anita? That tramp walks like she has a load of shit in her pants." I had never given Anita's gait much consideration, but on reflection I had to admit that my mother's description was apt.

My mother moved out, taking an apartment on the outskirts of Chapel Hill, and Anita moved in. For fall break, I had planned to stay in the dorms, but I changed my mind at the last minute and decided to surprise my mother. I arrived at her apartment, knocked on the door, and, when it opened, yelled, "Surprise!"—right into the face of a stranger. Either my mother had given me the wrong address or I had written it down wrong. The badly startled stranger let me use her phone, and I called my mother to apologize for not coming down.

"Have you been getting my letters?" I asked.

"No, I haven't."

"Are you sure? Maybe I have the address wrong." I read her what I had.

"That's the wrong apartment number," she said. Five minutes later I was at her door. "Wow," she said. "I was wondering why the connection sounded so good."

When I went home for the summer, Mike recruited me for one of his animal trips. The Albuquerque Zoo had offered a surplus Sumatran tiger for his pair of Siberians. Mike had planned to make the trip in the spring, but he had grown impatient after an occasion when he had darted the Siberians and he entered the cage before the sedatives had time to work fully. When the female had seen Mike approach the sleeping male, she had risen from her stupor and attacked. If she hadn't been sedated already, she probably would have killed him. As it was, she had torn deep gouges into his back and shoulder, dislocated his elbow, and ripped an ear before he crawled out of the cage. Fortunately, Mike knew a good ear surgeon.

Mike's daughter Annie accompanied us to Albuquerque. Anita was gone by then, and my mother agreed to watch the farm while we were away. Mike put the tigers' crates inside a horse trailer. Hauling a horse trailer filled with tigers around the country is complicated—you can't just pull into a roadside motel and park the truck for the night. The only places we could stay overnight safely were zoos. We made it to Memphis the first night. It was late, so I threw down my sleeping bag in the dark and went to sleep. I woke in the morning to the sound of a hippopotamus roaring about fifteen feet away. I have to say, there is nothing like the stench of hippo breath in the morning.

When we stopped for gas that morning, the pump jockey asked Mike what he had in the trailer.

59

"Tigers," said Mike.

"Nah. You telling me you got a tiger in there?"

"Two, actually."

"Y'all's kidding, right?" The man tried to peer through an opening in the trailer.

"You might want to step back," Mike cautioned.

But the man leaned even closer. Then the male Siberian charged, and the man jumped back as if he had caught a wrecking ball in the gut.

We made the Oklahoma City Zoo and Botanical Garden the next night, and Mike got a call from my mother. When my mother was leaving for work, she had found Engels, a young but very large tiger, playing on the woodpile in front of the house. Mike had built part of his cage out of particleboard to save money. Rain had weakened the particleboard, and Engels had punched his way through.

My mother had calmly gotten the tranquilizer gun, cleaned it, loaded it, and planted a dart in Engels' rump. After that, she called people to help put Engels back in his cage. She eventually got a local garage owner named Big Dee to help. When Big Dee had arrived, Engels had been just a tad bit sleepy, and the sight and sound of Big Dee's huge truck rolling into the yard sent him bolting over the fence and across the street. Big Dee was a veteran of the Siberian tiger fiasco and wanted nothing to do with the dart gun; he just wanted to shoot Engels with Mike's hunting rifle and be done with it. Barring that, he wanted to stay in his truck.

My mother called the sheriff next, and he and his deputies managed to find Engels, dart him again, and get him back in his cage.

My mother and Mike were trying to reconcile my sophomore year, so visits were often tumultuous. Once my mother came home after a date, grabbed a pair of scissors, and chopped off her hair.

Why did you do that? I asked.

She said, "Because Mike likes it long."

During one of my visits, I was sleeping on the living room couch around midnight when the front door flew open. I had gone to bed early because I had to return to college the next day, a fourteen-hour drive. My mother and Mike stormed in. Trailing behind them was an obviously terrified man I didn't recognize. After a few minutes of unintelligible screaming, Mike left. My mother went into her room and slammed the door, leaving me alone with the stranger. I made him a cup of coffee and extracted the story from him.

My mother had shipped her dog to New York to be bred. The breeder had decided the dog had a urinary tract infection and put her on the next plane home without consulting my mother. When my mother received a call that her dog had arrived, she had grabbed her checkbook and called Mike, and together they had headed for the Raleigh-Durham Airport, about forty minutes away.

No one had told my mother that the shipping company didn't take credit cards or personal checks, and my mother hadn't brought enough cash. This was back before cash machines. The clerks wouldn't release the dog without payment. It was Saturday, and the shipping office was closed Sunday, so they would have had to keep the dog until Monday.

My mother had erupted. "This isn't a crate full of goods! She can't just sit in the crate for another thirty-six hours, not with a bladder infection." Mike, being a man of action, had just taken the dog and loaded it into the van.

61

One of the clerks (the man now drinking coffee in my mother's dining room) had climbed in to stop them, but Mike had taken off. He had driven back to Chapel Hill so fast that there had been no way the clerk could exit safely.

"He wouldn't slow down," the clerk told me, still shaking. "Not even for the red lights."

I gave the man the phone to call his office. His office told him to wait. Twenty minutes later, the doorbell rang. Outside were two men, both over six feet tall and thick in the neck. Both were clearly armed. "We're with the State Bureau of Investigation," said the one in the brown corduroy shirt, flashing a badge. "Mind if we come in?"

It was one o'clock in the morning. Instead of getting a good night's sleep, I was hosting a kidnapping investigation.

In the presence of armed protectors, the clerk grew more assertive. My mother, meanwhile, was still incensed. "This is insane," she blared. "They could have told me they didn't accept checks or credit cards. There was no water in the crate and no food. If I had left her there overnight with her infection, she might have died."

I occupied the clerk while the SBI agents decided what to do. Locking up a woman who was trying to save her dog's life wouldn't serve anyone, and the real kidnapper, Mike, was long gone. Nobody seemed interested in tracking him down. They finally decided my mother could keep the dog. She agreed to be at her bank when it opened Monday morning. If she failed to show up at the freight office by ten o'clock Monday morning, the SBI would issue a warrant for her arrest on charges of kidnapping and theft.

Thomas Wolfe said you can't go home again, but my problem was that going home felt like . . . well, exactly like going home again. The question wasn't whether I could go home again. The question was: Why the hell would I?

Integrity

MY FIRST YEAR AT COLLEGE, I WAS ASSIGNED to a dorm known as the campus animal house. We residents had a huge water fight one of the first weeks, and the dean of students showed up in a raincoat and galoshes. Rushing water had turned the three flights of granite steps into a cataract, but he just stood at the bottom, holding an open umbrella over his head, and recited all the disciplinary actions that could be imposed on us if we didn't stop. This was something of an annual ritual for him.

I had been placed in a suite originally intended for two people. It had two small bedrooms off a sitting room. But the sitting room now housed two people, Angelo and David. Angelo's claim to fame was being able to name any rock song playing on the radio after hearing just four notes. David had mutton chop sideburns and played classical guitar. He was always ready with a rendition of "Classical Gas" when prompted. Needless to say, they were a bit of an odd couple.

Brian had the suite's other private room. He was a cherubic gay man with an acerbic wit. He was clearly looking forward to being out of the house and out of the closet. He whined nearly the entire year about being a virgin. By the end of the year, I think I wanted him to get laid even more than he did.

A smaller, two-room suite next door was a congregating place for campus radicals who played on an elite intramural basketball team called Spirit of Che. I came to think of them as the Clark Hall Commies. They played "Hurricane," Bob Dylan's protest against racism and injustice, incessantly.

The other end of the hall played only Steely Dan. One of the suites had a piece of paper on the outer door with a chart, labeled "Cal's pride chart." The chart was updated daily based on Cal's sexual activities and his roommate's assessment of the attractiveness of Cal's partners.

Across the hall was another three-room suite. In one of the private rooms was a huge man from Texas who claimed to have found god on an acid trip. He went home one break and hanged himself. Before his parents came to get his stuff, we purged his room of drugs and his huge collection of porn featuring extremely obese women.

The tenants of the former sitting room in this suite were Ananda and Joe. Joe was a real Carolina boy with an authentic accent, not a poseur like me. He played guitar and knew the words to almost every song John Prine ever recorded. Ananda was from Delhi, the son of a Bengali mother and African American father. He was teaching himself to play the sarod by listening to Amjad Ali Khan and Ali Akbar Khan repeatedly and playing along.

Ananda fascinated me to the point that I started following him around. One night he went to sit in the college chapel, and I slunk in and sat in a pew in the back. Later he let me know that he had seen me, which was incredibly embarrassing. I couldn't figure out what this was about—me, a straight man, stalking another man. In fact, it was years before I understood that it came down to my dysfunctional family, and the alternative Ananda represented.

Anita was not Mike's sole indiscretion when he was with my mother. One night, only a few months after I had moved to the farm, my mother and I came home and I was the first one out of the car. My sisters had stayed in town. I walked to the front door and reached for the knob, but I didn't actually touch it. I knew, just knew, that I couldn't open the door. Instead, I headed toward the cages to check on the animals.

My change of direction meant my mother was the first one through the door. The door slammed behind her, and from inside the trailer I heard screaming, first my mother and then Mike. After a while, the door opened, and a girl left. She lived nearby and was a frequent visitor to the farm. I figured she was about fourteen.

After more screaming, Mike came out, looking a little shaken and perhaps a bit contrite. We worked side by side, preparing meat for the cats on the tailgate of the pickup. "Your mother came in and caught us making out on the couch," he said with a tinge of remorse in his voice, but only a tinge. He didn't explain what he meant by "making out," but I was convinced he was talking about more than the kissing that often constituted making out in the eyes of my high school classmates. I imagined, perhaps intuited, what my mother saw while standing in the doorway—her partner screwing a fourteen-year-old girl.

"So what does this mean?" I asked.

"I don't know," he said.

In a surprisingly short amount of time, things seemed to return to normal. My mother did not leave. No one pressed charges. It was almost as if the whole thing never happened.

Although she never said so, I am convinced that my mom

was sleeping with Mike before my parents decided to separate. And that meant Mike was sleeping with my mom when she was one of his students and, because my mother worked in his lab, he was her supervisor. My father had quickly taken up with another woman, leaving my older sister and me alone in the house for long stretches. He eventually married this same woman, even though she clearly did not like his children and was not good at hiding her feelings.

Then there was Ananda. He had originally enrolled at Haverford but transferred to Wesleyan after refusing to sign an ethics pledge that included a promise to turn in any fellow student he caught cheating. He would pledge not to cheat but couldn't guarantee that no situation would ever arise where he might not turn in another student.

Between the Clark Hall Commies and Cal's pride chart, between the suicidal, porn-collecting Jesus freak and the vocally frustrated virgin, the dorm was a madhouse, but in the middle of this chaos, Ananda always seemed unperturbed and self-collected. Amid the cacophony of Angelo's radio, the Spirit of Che's Bob Dylan, the frat-boy wannabes' Steely Dan, Joe's John Prine, and David's Mason Williams, Ananda often sat almost motionless on the floor beside his bed with a headset on, legs crossed, eyes closed in concentration, playing the sarod so quietly it was almost inaudible.

I wasn't stalking him; I was stalking his integrity. It seemed to me an elusive, mystical creature I desperately wanted to capture and study. I had never experienced integrity in the people around me, and I needed to understand what it was, how it worked. If integrity was the pot of gold at the end of the rainbow, maybe Ananda was my leprechaun. Maybe if I followed him around long enough, he would lead me to it.

The Porn Store

AT NINETEEN I WAS DOING A LOT of things to challenge myself, to put myself in situations that took me outside my comfort zone. I wasn't concerned with doing the right thing, not yet; it seemed too early in life to presume to know with any certainty what was right and what was wrong. Instead, I was interested in exploring the boundaries of right and wrong, and a little experimentation—within limits—seemed justified. So, taking a job at the porn store fit right in.

It had started out as Brian's gig, but twenty hours a week was making it hard for him to keep up with his studies, and the manager agreed to a job share.

One or two companies controlled the porn trade in New England in the 1970s. Independent stores had a funny way of erupting in flames. I guess spontaneous combustion of pornographic materials is a known problem.

The adult bookstore in Middletown, Connecticut, was part of a chain run out of Providence, which, coincidentally, happened to be the seat of the New England mafia. Ownership stayed in the background, and managers were the public face of their shops. Like Brian's manager, George, they were often gay. About seventy percent of store purchases were made by gay men.

"Do you have any trouble being hit on by gays?" George asked during my interview.

Brian had told him I was straight. I said no.

"Good, because they are going to like you."

To be honest, I wasn't sure how far my basic acceptance of homosexuality would take me, but that, as much as anything else, is why I took the job. And I needed the money.

George was in his forties and obsessed with young men. He showed me brochures for a car he was thinking about buying. "What do you think?" he asked. I offered various comments about the car, none of which seemed to satisfy him. "But," he said finally, "if you were a high school boy, would you want to go for a ride in a car like that?"

A petite woman with long, dark hair came in one day and took in the store with her blue eyes. She was dressed like a professional just home from work. Being a woman made her an unusual customer, but the fact that she was unaccompanied made her unique. Women rarely came in except with their boyfriends, often reticently. She walked up to my perch behind the register and pointed to the glass case in front of me. "Can you help me pick out a vibrator?"

I was momentarily speechless and felt over my head. What did I possibly have to tell any woman about the benefits of one vibrator over another? I showed her one shaped like a tree that contorted itself, twisting as it vibrated. "The squirrel," I said, pointing to the rubber rodent at the base of the tree with its head reared, "is meant to vibrate against the clitoris." I actually said *clitoris*. *Clit* seemed too casual, too familiar.

I was afraid to ask her any of the questions that seemed to matter, questions about what she liked: How thick? How long? How much direct stimulation? Still, there was something intimate about the exchange. Customers asked me to go home with them all the time, and I just laughed, told them my girlfriend wouldn't like it. But for this woman I would have closed early or handed over keys to the customers and told them to make sure the last one out turned off the lights. But she didn't ask, of course, and I remained professional. She bought a simple vibrator—purple, plastic, no squirrels—and I went back to dusting the display of nitrate poppers.

Aside from that one visit, there was nothing titillating about the job. In fact, it was painfully boring. There is only so long I can look at porn. At best it is repetitive, uncreative, uninteresting, and depersonalized.

At closing time, I'd have to clean up the whole store before I could leave. This included the booths in the back that showed Super-8 loops. Cleaning the back required considerable care and attention to hygiene. The waste cans overflowed with tissues and paper towels; the floors were sticky and sometimes soaked with urine. I have no idea whether this was some form of fetish or a consequence of not letting customers use the employee toilet in the basement.

The store sucked the magic out of sex. After my regular evening shifts, I would have no interest in seeing my girlfriend.

Then the robbery happened.

From the beginning George had stressed the importance of following the rules. "The previous manager," he told me, "had epilepsy. He had a fit face-down in a puddle and drowned."

"You know," he concluded pointedly, "epileptic attacks can be induced."

George had bent the rules when he had agreed that Brian and I could train another student to work our shifts when we had too much schoolwork. It had to be a subcontracting arrangement, because Providence didn't like having to keep an eye on too many employees. Brian and I had to fill out our time cards as if we had worked the shift, and when we got paid, we paid the substitute.

The substitute was working during what would have been one of my shifts when a man walked in just before closing and shoved a large-caliber revolver in his face. The robber demanded the money from the till and then went into the back to collect the real money—all the quarters in the movie booths.

Since it had been my shift and the guy who was held up wasn't officially on the payroll, I debriefed him and told the police that I had been working during the robbery. A few days later, a station wagon with Rhode Island plates pulled up. A large, muscular man came in, walked up to the counter, and asked me my name. Another man of similar size positioned himself just inside the front door and watched the street. We were alone. It was clear that I was not allowed to leave, and no one else would be allowed to enter.

The man at the counter began grilling me about the robbery. I could see the outline of a gun under his jacket. "The guy knew the operation," he said when he had exhausted his list of questions. "He knew when to hit and where the money would be. Sounds like a former employee."

His final words were, "I have some ideas. Don't worry, we'll find him."

To this day, I am certain he found the robber and equally certain that I never want to know what happened after that.

The visit forced me to deal with the morality not of pornography but of where my paycheck was coming from. For some inexplicable reason, lying to an armed mafia enforcer made me nervous.

I quit soon afterward. It was easy to do, because people figured I was shaken up by the robbery, but really I was shaken up by something else.

One night my housemates woke well after midnight to the sound of a woman sobbing on the sidewalk. They rushed to check on her and learned that she had accepted a ride home from a bar from a man she knew slightly. The man had taken her to a deserted road and raped her, then he had dropped her off near our house. My housemates went with her to the hospital, where a member of the emergency room staff said to her, "What is it this time?" The police were equally unsympathetic and demanded to know why she had accepted a ride. "It was like watching her being raped all over again," said one of my housemates.

I slept through this, but the next day the household met, and we concluded our town needed a sexual-assault crisis-intervention center. We agreed the first step was for one of us to go through the training at the closest center, which was in Hartford. We checked the schedule of trainings, and most of us weren't available. In the end, I was chosen and signed up for the summer training. Which is how, in a matter of months, I went from selling porn to answering a rape-crisis line.

There is such a thing as being outside your comfort zone, and then there is being outside the realm of what is justifiable or even conceivable. I think it takes a lot of hubris for one person to claim to be an expert on what's right and what's wrong, but the great thing about growing up is that eventually, if you are lucky, you start to figure out what is right for you.

He Makes Me Laugh

AFTER COLLEGE, I MOVED TO Albuquerque with my girlfriend, Rachel. I was going to graduate school because I didn't know what else to do. I had a hard time finding work in the middle of the Reagan recession, and I did not like my graduate program. My senior year at college, I had found my niche as a campus activist. I had always been something of a misfit, but for a time I really felt like I belonged. And I was in love. Suddenly all that was gone: I had no friends, no sense of purpose, and Rachel and I started having problems.

Rachel was an amazing woman—a writer, an artist, and wicked-ass smart. She was a freshman and I was a senior when we met, and I am not sure when I found out that she had graduated high school two years early. I had to do the math at one point to determine that I had not committed statutory rape. When we moved to Albuquerque, I was twenty-two and she was seventeen. She was young, and I was terribly immature.

You can imagine how she must have felt: smart, precocious, anxious to experience the world, anxious to figure out how she fit in. Yet here she was, playing house in a new town where she

73

had no friends and her only companion was an increasingly morose and clingy boyfriend.

One day she complained, "We only make love once a day. We used to make love at least twice a day." Another time she told me our lovemaking was "too predictable, like we've become friends and are just going through the motions." I focused on the "too predictable" part and conveniently ignored the part about "just friends." I figured I could fix it, right? More sex. More variety. That was easy. But of course it wasn't easy at all. Everything I tried just made things worse.

We both volunteered at Agora, a campus crisis-intervention line, and that spring Agora held its annual retreat. At one workshop, an art therapist paired us up with people we didn't know well and asked us to study our partner and then draw our impression of him or her using colors and patterns only, no shapes, figures, or words.

I was stunned when Rachel's partner, a man named Daryl, showed his impression of her. It is a swirl of reds and oranges. It portended a future I had already sensed but until that moment had been able to deny. I saw a Rachel in turmoil, full of passion and about to erupt. The truth of that image terrified me beyond comprehension.

"There's a lot of sexual tension in there," I said to Rachel after the workshop. She dismissed my comment, but as the day passed into evening, I grew increasingly jealous. It was a pathetic, desperate form of jealousy, unlike anything I had experienced, and all because of a silly crayon scribble. That night there was a party. I felt queasy, unstable. I wanted Rachel's reassurance, but she ignored me, and eventually I went back to our tiny room, where I curled up in a fetal position and sobbed.

Two weeks later I was at work and could feel myself growing agitated. I had an overwhelming need to go home. As the shift supervisor at a car-rental place, I could be fired for leaving the premises. I struggled with this compulsion as long as I could, and then jumped into a rental and raced home. I had no idea why I was there, but like a robot under remote control I walked into the house and made a beeline for the bathroom. I opened a drawer, the one in which Rachel kept her diaphragm, and it was gone.

Years later, when we were able to talk about it, I found out she had had a crush on Daryl before the retreat and had gone to the party wanting to seduce him. The day I raced home, she had gone to meet him. She had left the house at exactly the same time I had left work. They had tried sex, but both were ambivalent, and he had been impotent. The spell had been broken. She told me she had hoped that if she could get in touch with her passion again, even if it was with another man, maybe things would get better between us.

Later, she had a similar attraction to another man, a workmate of mine named Danny. I couldn't understand the attraction, and when I asked her about it, she said, "He makes me laugh." And, of course, I remembered all the times I had made her laugh.

Rachel went back to college in Connecticut that fall. We had agreed to a one-year separation, but I did not wait a year. I dropped out of class and headed east. The first night, I dreamed of someone in bed with Rachel. He had his back to me. Every night before I reached Connecticut, I had the same dream. Each night the man turned a little bit more in my direction, but still I couldn't see his face. When I got there, I pressed Rachel about the dreams. I expected that she was seeing someone, but when I found out that the someone was Michael, one of my best friends from college, the dreams made sense.

To say those were painful weeks would be an understatement. I won't go into the details, but you can imagine. I think the loss of one of my few friendships hurt as much as anything else. At some point Rachel decided she wanted to be just with me, but then she started to equivocate. One night I came home late from work in Hartford, and my route took me past Michael's house. Rachel's car was in his driveway.

I felt like I was losing my grip on reality. Supposedly Rachel and Michael were not lovers anymore, but I couldn't bear to go back to my Albuquerque state of mind, when I struggled to sort out what was real and what wasn't. After Daryl's drawing, after the mad dash home from work, after the dreams, I was confused. There were the things Rachel was telling me and then there were the things I knew, just knew without any evidence, and they didn't match up. I needed a reality fix. I needed a signpost, like one of those rural road signs that people like to shoot up. The sign didn't need to be bulletproof; it just needed to feel solid.

I went up to the house. I couldn't see anything through the downstairs window, but Michael's bedroom light was on. I didn't decide to climb the railing and shimmy onto the porch roof; I just did it.

Rachel was seated on Michael's bed. He was shirtless. She was clothed and giving him a back rub. They seemed so comfortable with each other. Her touch was gentle. Their conversation flowed easily. Even during our struggles, Rachel and I had had small moments like this, but not lately. It seemed so unfair that there were three of us in this little passion play, yet they had sacrificed nothing, while I was literally out in the cold.

Then Michael said something that made Rachel laugh. Albuquerque came back to me. Danny came back to me: "He makes me laugh." And I lost it. I smashed my first through the

76

storm window. As I climbed down from the roof, I left a trail of blood from my lacerated hand on the white support posts.

Rachel was first out of the house. She will be furious, I thought. My actions were inexcusable. But amazingly, she ran toward me, looking concerned. "Are you hurt?" she asked.

Michael offered no such sympathy. He was irate. "You were up on my roof? You have no right! You'll pay for that window!"

I ignored him. Rachel cupped my bloody hand in hers and led me away in the direction of my house. I was shocked at my own behavior and in total disbelief that Rachel was comforting me.

Michael was still screaming, waving his arms around in the air. "We weren't doing anything, damn it! We weren't doing anything!" By which he meant they weren't having sex.

Although it was not clear to me—and was most likely not clear to them, either—where the back rub might have led, I knew full well they weren't having sex. I was on the other side of the glass, after all.

But it was not true that they were not doing anything. They were doing a lot. They were communicating. They were enjoying each other. They were laughing. And to me that didn't feel like nothing.

It felt like everything.

More Human Than Most People

FOR SPRING BREAK MY JUNIOR YEAR, Tief and I went home to my mother's apartment. I was sunning myself when a young woman heading home from the pool ran straight toward me. To Tief, she was a stranger racing through his yard, bearing down on his owner. He lunged at her, pushing her out of the way. I grabbed Tief and apologized. She said she was fine and kept going.

Soon, though, she was back with a furious boyfriend. He pointed to a speck of blood on her back, just above the top of her bikini bottom. Tief's claws had slightly broken her skin, but now the pair insisted he had bitten her and demanded proof that Tief was vaccinated. He was, but we couldn't prove it. Tigers get rabies, too, and it is hard to find a vet willing to walk into a tiger compound to administer a shot. So a friendly vet had provided the vaccine and let Mike take care of it. No muss, no fuss, no bills—but also no documentation.

The boyfriend insisted on calling the animal-control officer, who showed up looking like a Southern sheriff out of Hollywood central casting. He wore his hair in a crew cut, his few remaining teeth were brown from chewing tobacco, and an ample paunch hung over his belt.

"I came as fast as I could when I heard it was a bouvier," he said immediately. "I couldn't believe it when they told me. A bouvier would never bite unprovoked." I explained my version of events, which reconfirmed his faith in the breed.

"I'm real sorry, y'all, but I'm going to have to quarantine him for two weeks. Normally you'd have to put him up at a vet's and pay the boarding fee. That'll cost. But I'll tell y'all what. Seeing as how it's a bouvier and all, you can put him up at my place. I'll charge you four or five bucks a day just to cover the cost of his food."

My sister Gwenn and I rode over to his place in his truck. The prisoner rode in the back. Being the county animal-control officer was part-time work. Our host earned the rest of his living training guard dogs. He had been with the K-9 Corps in the Pacific during the war, and his life's ambition, he told us, was to save up enough money to buy a bouvier.

He lived in a rundown farmhouse surrounded by kennels occupied by a mix of dogs, mostly dobermans and rottweilers. I asked him if he thought the kennels would hold Tief. They all had dirt floors, and most had open tops.

"Don't see why not. I've had every kind of dog imaginable in these kennels over the years. Ain't a one ever got out." It didn't seem to matter when I told him that Tief's uncle was in the Guinness Book of World Records for climbing a chain-link fence, or that we had nicknamed Tief Houdini because of his ability to escape from almost anything.

"C'mon," he said after latching Tief in. "I got something I want to show you." He went into his house and returned with a stack of books. Every single one was about bouviers. We spent the next twenty minutes looking through the books and trading bouvier stories before going back to check on Tief, who had been digging during our absence. His escape was only a matter of time.

"See here," said our new best friend, "I ain't supposed to do this, but seeing as how it's a bouvier and all, y'all can take him home. I'll come by a couple times to make sure he ain't dead or frothing at the mouth or nothing."

Classes were starting, so I had to leave Tief at my mother's. The dogcatcher never did stop by. I suspect he believed that Tief was immune to rabies, seeing as how he was a bouvier and all.

Having left Tief for a few months during his supposed rabies quarantine, it was easier to leave him in North Carolina while I was in New Mexico. My mother was back on the farm with Mike by then, and Tief was comfortable there. I had been in Albuquerque less than a year when my mother called with news about Tief. It had taken her weeks to work up the courage.

"I took Tief in to Wally's for surgery because his abscess seemed to be getting worse," she told me.

Wally was our vet at the time. Tief was a monorchid, a one-balled dog. His second testicle never descended. An undeveloped testicle can become cancerous, and my mother had wanted to have it removed. The breeder we bought Tief from had been adamant that the surgical risks were greater than the cancer risks, and I had been inclined to trust him, but my mother had gone ahead and scheduled the operation with a vet who was not Wally. The surgery had been more complicated than expected, and the surgeon, in an act of veterinary malpractice, had sewn him up with fishing line to save a few dollars. The wound had never healed properly. Tief had sometimes whimpered uncomfortably and licked the small opening in his belly, but otherwise he had seemed fine. The fact that Tief had had surgery was news to me, but my mother had more to say.

She went on to tell me that Wally had called her after the surgery. "I don't know what's wrong with Tief," he had said, "but we can't get him to settle down. I think he wants to go home." So my mother had gone and picked him up. Once home, Tief had settled in the corner of the family room, clearly uncomfortable but calm.

"After a while, he got up, walked over to me, licked my face, placed his head in my lap, and closed his eyes," my mother told me. "The other dogs were all outside, but when Tief closed his eyes, they immediately began to howl. And they continued to howl for hours."

I later learned that my mother had put Tief through a series of surgeries, and the surgeries had weakened his intestinal wall. A postmortem exam showed that his intestinal wall had ruptured. I believe Tief knew he was dying and had decided to die at home. He wanted to say good-bye.

There was a large, fenced pit in the back pasture of the farm for disposing of dead animals, but my mother couldn't bring herself to put Tief's body in the pit, so she buried him in a grave among the weathered and fallen headstones of the people who had once farmed the land. "He was more human than most of the people I know," she explained.

For a long time, I didn't talk about Tief's death very much. I felt guilty about leaving him behind, about not standing up to my mother when she insisted on the first surgery, about not being around to object to the other surgeries, and mostly about not being there when he died. Once I told the story to a group of people in the living room of my friend Miriam's house. At that time, she shared a basement bedroom with her two dogs.

One of them was Arnie, a stocky, muscular beast named after Arnold Schwarzenegger. Arnie didn't like many people, and he didn't know me at all, but as I finished the story in tears, we heard claws scraping on the door to the basement. When Miriam opened the door, Arnie walked out, came straight over to me, licked my face, then turned around and went back downstairs. As she closed the basement door, Miriam looked at me curiously and said, "He almost never comes upstairs."

Uncle Mack's Passing

I AM ALWAYS INTERESTED IN THE CHANGES that result when people's paths intersect. How one person's passage through another person's life shifts things, sometimes in dramatic ways and sometimes in ways so subtle that we never notice. Whether we are aware of it or not, we all leave bread crumbs to mark the ways we have traveled.

For example, I used to have a girlfriend who chewed with her mouth open until I pointed it out to her. We are still friends. I doubt she remembers my comment or her former behavior, and I have never brought it up. It might have been embarrassing for both of us—I mean, it was rude of me to point it out and neurotic of me to care—but when we get together, I love watching her eat. It makes me happy. The fact that she chews with her mouth closed is proof that I exist and have an impact.

It's a bread crumb.

My Uncle Mack wasn't really my uncle. He was Mike's uncle, which made him my step-great-uncle. When Mack retired, Mike invited him to live with us. Mack would tell people, "I worked for Rocky," which meant he had been a building inspector for the state of New York when Nelson Rockefeller was governor.

Mack resembled a chimpanzee. His sinewy arms reached almost to his knees, and he walked with his narrow shoulders hunched forward and his legs slightly bent. Plus, he had no butt whatsoever and had to keep tightening his belt to prevent his jeans from falling down.

He smoked Antonio Y Cleopatra cigars, constantly chewing on the plastic tips. When a person did something he disliked, he was apt to say, "That man's from hunger." I was never sure what that meant, but I have a hunch it was an ethnic slur, possibly a holdover from Russia where he was born. He ate the same thing every morning for breakfast: one hard-boiled egg and two slices of white bread washed down with a cup of hot water. "It's not the caffeine in coffee or tea that wakes you up," he insisted. "It's the warmth." Though a fairly tall man, he pulled the seat of his bronze Valiant as far forward as it could go and drove hunched over, his chest almost touching the wheel.

"Never look in the rearview mirror," he told me more than once when he was teaching me to drive. "What's behind you doesn't matter."

Mack was crotchety, but he always had time for me. He obviously wasn't cut out to be a driving instructor, but he made himself available, and he had faith in me. I told him once that I got a poor grade on a test because I was lazy, meaning I didn't study. "You're not lazy," he said. I truly believed that my poor study habits were just one manifestation of a defining character deficit, but he rejected that idea with such conviction that I had to rethink things. After a careful self-inventory, I decided he was right. I had some bad habits, but at my core I was not a lazy person.

Mack's arrival meant we needed more room, and he helped finance an expansion of the old farmhouse. That gave us plenty of bedrooms for our blended family and more room to raise animals in the house. One of those animals was a young male lion whose cage was an upside-down crate on the back porch. One day Uncle Mack let the crate drop on his tail, which is how we ended up with a tailless lion. Because of his injury, I ended up bonding with the lion. When we moved him to an outside cage, I visited frequently, trying to figure out how to be a lion tamer. I sucked, frankly—mostly the cub would jump me, and we would wrestle—but I tried.

After I left for college, Mack bought a place in a Fort Lauderdale retirement community. My senior year, Rachel and I went down to visit him and ran into an ice storm on the way back. Three deer froze in the headlights, and I did an amazing piece of driving: I missed two out of three. When I said we should bleed the third and take it home for my mom to cook, this upset Rachel, who was a vegetarian. The rest of the trip was a heated debate about the merit of eating meat. Finally, Rachel said there was no point in arguing because I was too stubborn, but that was January 1979, and I haven't eaten meat since. It is a stretch, I know. I became a vegetarian because of Rachel, but without Mack, I never would have been in that storm, never would have hit that deer. My diet is another of Mack's bread crumbs.

In that cold winter in Connecticut, after Rachel and I finally stopped trying, I worked as a canvasser, doing door-to-door fund-raising for the Connecticut Citizens Action Group. It was a confusing time. Constantly trying to reconcile what I was being told with what I was sensing had contributed to the breakup being far more destructive than was necessary. I hadn't believed in myself, and I had tried to believe all of Rachel's assertions while also blindly ignoring many of the important things she kept trying to tell me. I desperately needed to figure out where knowledge comes from, which truths were true.

One very cold night, I was canvassing in one of the quaint suburban towns that ring Hartford. I was close to raising my nightly quota, and the night was bitterly cold, so I found myself wishing someone would ask me in. At the next door I knocked on, the home owner invited me to join a birthday party. The birthday boy was a radio psychic. People called into his nationally syndicated show, and he told them his psychic impressions of their lives. "I always knew I was different," he told me, "even as a small child." Except for his stories and how he made his living, nothing seemed remarkable about this man.

He focused on me at one point and said, "You've recently lost a member of your family." This made no sense to me at all. "He wasn't really a member of your family," he continued, "but he was treated as one. He lived with you for a while, but not at the end. You were closer to him than the others."

I thought about this for a while and decided he must be talking about Tief. He had felt like a member of the family, even though he was a dog. He had lived with me for about six years, but he died at the farm while I was in Albuquerque. And since he was my dog, I was certainly closer to him than the other members of my family. Tief had been dead about a year, so I suppose his death could have been considered recent.

I left impressed but not overwhelmed. The next time I spoke to my mother, though, she informed me, belatedly, that Uncle Mack had passed away about a month before. She just hadn't gotten around to calling me.

The radio psychic could not have read my mind or taken cues from my body language; with uncanny accuracy he had told me of an event I had not even learned about myself. Now, I was impressed, but I was also reassured somehow. The door I wouldn't open, Daryl's drawing of Rachel, the empty bathroom drawer, the dreams, and hundreds of other moments in my life seemed less freaky all of a sudden. I would never be a national radio psychic, but believing in this guy made it easier to believe in myself.

Sometimes I wonder if this was Uncle Mack's last bread crumb, a gift from beyond the grave. As if he had used the psychic to tell me, with conviction, "You're not crazy."

I owe a lot to Mack. Without him, I would have never been able to say that I am a productive, motivated, highly intuitive vegetarian and former lion tamer. He was, however, wrong about one thing:

What's behind you does matter.

The Cloak of Nessus

I AM NOT THE KIND OF STORYTELLER who retells classical myths, but this once I will make an exception, because this particular myth is personal.

This is the story of Hercules, his bride Deianira, and a centaur named Nessus.

Nessus was a ferryman who carried Deianira and Hercules across the river on the newlyweds' journey home. Because Hercules had earlier driven Nessus from his home, Nessus took advantage of the situation. There are different accounts of this myth. Some say Nessus insulted Deianira when he carried her on his back; some say he tried to rape her. Either way, Hercules shot Nessus with his bow. As Nessus lay dying, he whispered his last words to Deianira. According to one version, he told her that if Hercules ever needed help, she should send her husband the centaur's blood-soaked cloak for protection.

Needless to say, there came a time when Deianira thought her husband might need the cloak, and so she sent it to him. The cloak, however, was tainted with hydra toxin, which apparently is a very bad thing. As soon as Hercules wrapped the bloodstained cloak around himself, his body began to feel as if it was on fire. He could not remove the cloak. The agony would have killed anyone else, but Hercules was part god, the son of Zeus. So he lived and returned home to find that his wife had killed herself when she heard about the suffering created by her foolish gift.

Pining and in unrelenting pain, Hercules had a great funeral pyre built, lay down on it, and ordered it lit. Such was the end of his days on Earth. It was the gift of blood, a gift given with the intent of doing good, that caused Hercules's downfall.

Which brings me back to my own story.

In January 1985 I got an unxpected and very scary phone call Susan, the nurse coordinator of the Hemophilia Treatment Center in San Francisco. She was also a friend. We occasionally had dinner together, and when she traveled, I took care of her house and her two springer spaniels.

She called to suggest that I take a blood test that would detect antibodies to the human immunodeficiency virus. "We are testing everybody," she said. "Just about everyone is positive. I think you should prepare yourself."

I was cocky. I used less of the blood-derived anti-hemophilia medicine than my peers. I was healthier, more active. I still had a jump shot, still went backpacking. Things like this didn't happen to me, even if they happened to other hemophiliacs. I had always been lucky, and I believed I always would be. I told Susan I would be happy to take her test.

After I hung up, I wondered how things could have changed so quickly. How could a rare disease restricted almost exclusively to gay men and people who shared needles spread so quickly that Susan was now convinced that I had been exposed? There were reports of hemophiliacs contracting AIDS, sure, but how could public health experts extrapolate from twenty-one cases a year ago to an assumption that several thousand people had almost certainly been infected?

Less than fifteen months before Susan's call, the highly respected hematologist Dr. Margaret Hilgartner—Dr. H to her patients, her hematology colleagues, and my sister, who interned in her lab—had declared at a National Hemophilia Foundation meeting that the chance of contracting AIDS from anti-hemophilia drugs was a million to one. With my luck and my history, I thought, I could live with those odds.

I went to the hospital. Susan drew my blood. I got back to my life. Denial is a powerful thing. But several days later, when I returned a message from Susan, my confidence was beginning to wane.

"Hi, Susan, it's Craig." I noticed a slight warble in my voice. "Do you have the results?"

"I do. They're inconclusive."

"What does that mean?"

"It means we run it again. I'm sure you've been exposed."

There were many things I didn't know at the time—things Susan probably did know. I didn't know, for example, that several months before Susan's call, the Centers for Disease Control had reported that a third to a half of the hemophiliacs tested had abnormally low levels of a class of immune cells called T-cells and were expected to develop AIDS. I didn't know that six months earlier, antibody testing of a sample group of hemophiliacs had revealed that 72 percent had been exposed to HIV. These findings had not been widely disseminated.

The second test was inconclusive as well, so Susan ordered a different kind of test, one considered more sensitive. The results bore her out, but all that meant was that I was positive for antibodies. It was possible that the virus had been deactivated during the manufacturing process. It was possible I had developed antibodies to inactive fragments of the virus, to dead viruses, to live viruses that had been crippled in some way, or to live viruses in such small quantities that my body had been able to fight off infection.

Susan offered a possible way to get answers. She explained that when you culture the blood of people with HIV, it produces higher than normal levels of a particular enzyme. The test would take about a week, she said. When I called in for my results, her answer was one I had heard before: inconclusive. "Your blood produces more of the enzyme than most people," she explained, "but not nearly the level that we are finding in other people with HIV."

We agreed to continue the culture. A couple weeks went by before the culture failed and I got the results from Susan. "As long as we kept the culture alive," she said, "the enzyme level kept going up. That suggests there's live virus in the culture." Live virus, but I was somehow different than people with AIDS, or even most people with HIV infection. I held on to the hope that my virus was a less virulent strain, too weak to give me AIDS. Susan passed on a comment by the doctor overseeing the test: "He's not one of the ones we need to worry about."

That was reassuring, but needless to say I worried, and eventually denial became impossible. As the science improved, doctors were able to identify the virus living in my blood.

In hindsight, the one-in-a-million figure cited by Dr. H in 1983 was unjustifiable. By the start of that year, six U.S. hemophiliacs had died of AIDS, fourteen were known to have the disease and another ten were suspected of having the disease. The U.S. population of people with hemophilia was 15,000, but many were people with mild cases who rarely required treatment. That hardly would be one in a million—in fact, it sounds on the surface like closer to one in a few hundred—unless someone was prepared to argue that the infected hemophiliacs were all gay or users of intravenous street drugs, were exposed in some other, as-yet-undiscovered manner, or had that world's most damnable luck. Dr. H apparently didn't do the math. And as late as 1985, physicians were still prescribing the tainted factor to hemophiliacs who had never been exposed before, even though older, far less risky treatments were available.

This is how I came to wear the cloak of Nessus. People like Susan thought they were helping when they offered me the gift of blood. They had meant well. Dr. Hilgartner and her colleagues hadn't played the role of Nessus, not really; they were more like Deianira.

When I think about the story of Nessus, it's not Hercules who evokes the greatest sense of pathos. I am much more affected by Deianira's story, by the well-meaning but profoundly naive wife who killed herself out of guilt. I think about the Deianiras of my world who thought they were doing the right thing, who thought they were keeping me safe, until the day came when they had to start making those calls.

What were they feeling when they picked up the phone? And what burdens do they carry still?

The Fox Demon

IN THE SUMMER OF **1986,** eighteen months after my HIV diagnosis, my friend Susan said she wanted to drive to Seattle, following Highway 1 up the coast. "I don't have anyone to go with," she said, "but if I have to, I'll go alone." That was all the invitation I needed.

We spent the first night in Arcata, and the next day we drove up Route 1 until we found a beach that would be perfect for the next event on our itinerary. The parking lot was full, but the day was windy and breezy, and people were sticking close to their vehicles.

In a clear patch of dry sand on the far end of the beach, we settled down out of the wind and out of sight of the parking lot. Reaching into her pocket, Susan brought out a bag of gelatin capsules filled with white powder. "I find that one usually isn't enough," she said. "I start with one and a half. When I start to feel the drug wear off, I take the other half, just to stretch the trip out a bit."

Ecstasy had just been outlawed, but it was still widely used by therapists. Though it was showing up more and more at parties, some people saw it as a tool for personal growth. Susan was one of those people.

I had never tried it, but I knew it was working when I realized I was free from anxiety. The wind no longer nagged at me. Sunburn wasn't a problem because I had made peace with the sun the way a firewalker makes peace with the coals. I wasn't concerned that some tourist might guess what we were up to. And I stopped worrying about the gear in Susan's car, which had a busted trunk lock. What I remember most was a feeling of safety. It was the perfect afternoon on the perfect beach with the perfect companion, and there was nothing that needed to be done except to enjoy every moment.

When the drug wore off, the feeling of perfection ended. My body had metabolized the drug into toxins that raided my stores of essential vitamins and minerals. My mouth was dry, and I couldn't stop flexing my jaw. I was tired, very tired. Susan settled me into the passenger seat, found a campground, fed me tuna sandwiches, and cleaned up while I crawled into my sleeping bag. Within minutes I was dreaming. My Continental Airlines flight to La Guardia was landing at the TWA terminal at Newark.

That was the last good rest I had for days. I found it hard to sleep when the dreams came. The basic plot was always the same. I desperately needed to get somewhere—where, exactly, was never clear—and was constantly thwarted. The shuttle wouldn't take me to my connecting flight; the southbound train headed north out of the station; the downtown local turned into an uptown express. I initially considered the dreams unimportant, but in hindsight the clues were there: the repetition, the vividness, the sense of frustration that forced me awake, and the way the dreams refused to fade.

94

Our days were largely uneventful. In a small coastal town, a dog ran across the road in front of us. We barely missed it, and the incident shook us both. When we reached Seattle, we got lost. Numbered streets and numbered avenues wove in and out of one another.

On the first day of our return trip, we took a detour up into the mountains and found a campsite on the shore of a small lake. There my dreams began to change. In one, I sat at a table with a group of coworkers. On the table lay a birthday cake decorated with the face of a clown. We had been waiting for the boss to show up so that we could begin. "We have to wait," said one coworker. "He'll be really angry," said another. Then I surprised myself by driving my hand into the middle of the clown's face. My fist came away full of cake, and I shoved it into my mouth. A cheer went up around the table, and I woke up laughing. The elation was so electrifying that it took me nearly half an hour to fall asleep again.

The second dream began on the edge of a lake. There was to be a picnic, and our meal was cooking in a Franklin stove. "What's inside?" I asked.

"A goose," someone answered. "They're cooking a goose."

A small animal appeared at the water's edge. It wasn't quite like anything I had seen before. It might have been a fox or a weasel or a dog. Whatever it was, it went to the stove, pushed open the door with its snout, and dragged out the goose. I grabbed a gun from someone nearby and fired. The bullet made the one fox explode into more than a dozen foxes, all of which turned on me and began to nip, shredding my pants and tearing skin from my ankles.

I jumped into a car and drove away along a dirt road. I knew I'd be all right if I could get to the highway. In the distance I could see the glow of a Waffle Shop sign, a sure indica-

95

tor of a highway interchange, but I couldn't find a way to cut over. I was lost again. Suddenly the original fox appeared in the middle of the road. I didn't have time to stop and wasn't sure that I wanted to. The car jolted as it struck the fox, and I heard bones break under the wheels. When I came to a stop, I turned to look back.

Until that point in my life, I had never noticed whether I dream in color. Some people do and some don't. I do. The moonlit sky was purple. The trees that lined the road were a green so deep they were almost black. The fox glowed a reddish orange as it rested on its haunches in the middle of the yellow road, and the eyes that taunted me were a brilliant, piercing green. In front of the fox was a crumpled human shape; it wasn't white so much as without color, like a shadow in a photographic negative. Beside this shape lay a cane. The only other thing in the scene that didn't have a color was the scream that echoed off the night sky as I awoke.

A couple weeks later, when I told Susan about the dream, she asked, "So who did you run over? Who was in the road?"

I told her I was pretty sure it was my father.

She took a sip of beer before asking the one question that mattered right then. "Does your father use a cane?"

As I answered no, a shudder passed through me—dread combined with the same elation I felt when I smashed the birthday cake. I knew where I had to get to. That place that was so hard to find. That place the boss didn't want me to see. The place that was too scary to visit before the ecstasy weakened my fear.

I knew who lay dead in the road. At that point in my life, my left knee was really bothering me. I was using a cane.

In that moment, I truly confronted my own death for the first time.

The following weeks were some of the best of my life. I woke up enthused about each new day. I exercised, ate healthy meals, and lost weight. I contacted old friends whose phone calls and letters had gone unanswered for far too long.

Susan wasn't finished with me, though. In September she called to say that the Berkeley Art Museum was featuring a show of Francesco Clemente, and she wondered whether I would like to go. Clemente didn't make much of an impression on me, so I wandered off and entered an exhibit called *Japanese Ghosts and Demons: Art of the Supernatural.*

I was drawn immediately to "New Year's Eve Foxfires at the Changing Tree," a 19th century print by Andō Hiroshige. The work is a representation of fox demons, or *kitsune*, common figures in Japanese folklore. A wall plaque explained that the fox demon is a trickster figure, and one role of the trickster is to force us to understand and accept aspects of ourselves that we might otherwise deny.

In the foreground of the print was a tree, and under the tree glowed more than a dozen stylized animals, each identical to the ones in my dream.

Passing on Curves

WHEN I AM IN THE WOODS for more than a day or two, everything slows down. I stop talking; I enter a trancelike state. My friends once made the mistake of letting me drive home like that. I was on a narrow, winding highway, a cliff face on one side and a steep drop on the other, making good time despite heavy truck traffic, when my girlfriend looked over and said, placidly, "I trust you. I know you know what's around the bend. But some of us might be more comfortable if you didn't pass on the curves."

This is a story about passing on curves.

As a child with hemophilia, I was told constantly about what I couldn't do. I learned to ignore limitations. I learned to trust my instincts. Curves, road signs, trucks, double yellow lines mean nothing to me. So when I was diagnosed with HIV in 1985, I just kept driving. I went to graduate school, launched a new career, got married . . . and I had a child.

My daughter was conceived in the back seat of a car. Unfortunately, I was in the front seat at the time. While I watched for passersby, my wife, Karen, performed highly unerotic acts involving a syringe and a Gerber baby food jar containing donated sperm.

Karen was convinced she was carrying a boy, so we had not decided on a girl's name, though we had considered naming the kid after Karen's grandmother. When my daughter was born blue, with her umbilical cord wrapped twice around her neck, when the midwife looked up from between my wife's legs and said "she's floppy," I used the only girl's name I had, the grandmother's name, to call my daughter back into this world, and since she answered, she became, irrevocably, Manya.

We had a plan, my wife and I. I would hold on until Manya was in kindergarten, making it easier for Karen to work and not have to cover huge day-care costs. And then I would die. It was a good plan. Obviously, though, I knew nothing about being a parent. A few weeks after the birth, I was sitting in a friend's kitchen, staring out the window, when it hit me: It's not about me anymore. The foundations of my life were suddenly swept away, and yet I found myself planted even more firmly on the ground.

Manya had a hard time falling asleep. She had too many questions. She was maybe two when she called me into her room during nap time. Standing up in her crib, she pointed toward the window. "What dat?" she demanded.

"The window?"

"No, what dat?"

"The curtains?"

"No, what dat?"

I looked out the window. "The tree?"

"Not dat," she said, pointing at the window, "and not dat," pointing now at the mattress of her crib. "What dat?", pointing somewhere in between. And then I got it. "That," I said, smiling, "is air." I couldn't explain what air was, but at least now she had a name for the nothing.

Next she wanted to know, "Daddy, who were the first mommy and daddy's mommy and daddy?" Think about it. It's a great question.

When she was three, she asked, "Daddy, why are we here?" None of my answers fully satisfied her, but I told her what she was experiencing was called existential angst and if she was lucky it would go away in her late twenties. Now, she could name her anxiety. I would be driving and from the backseat of the car she would tell me, "Daddy, I have existential angst."

The more I understood what it meant to be a father, the more I understood my hubris. This kid loved me in a way I had never been loved before, and that was mind-blowing enough, but she also needed me, trusted me. She wanted to shake the world like a snow globe so she could watch all that knowledge fall down from the sky and settle at her feet. And she counted on me to be there, to be both her sidekick and her superhero. But I was going to leave her.

For the first time in my life, it seemed, I hadn't known what was around the bend.

She called me in one night to ask, "Daddy, is Elmo a good monster or a bad monster?"

Finally, a question I could answer. "Elmo is a good monster." I turned to leave, but she wasn't done.

"Daddy, will you keep me safe from the bad monsters?"

I turned back and said, "Of course I will."

How could I say anything else? But it was a lie. The monster was already in the house . . . I had brought it in.

The lie hit me so hard that I began to have regrets about my choice to parent. But those regrets caused a great deal of dissonance. How could I regret the decision that produced my wonderful child?

In 1996, I read in the paper about success treating HIV with a new drug, Crixivan, the first protease inhibitor. I put my head down on the table and sobbed, repeating aloud to an empy house, "I might live. I might live. I might live."

I began to believe I could get away with it one more time, this passing on curves. But I hadn't yet spotted the other truck, the one coming from Karen's direction. It first manifested as a scattering of spots on a mammogram, then later as roughly fifty positive lymph nodes. At the same time, information was coming out about the HIV virus developing resistance to the new drugs.

Suddenly Manya had two parents with fatal illnesses. All three of us were in the same car, rushing headlong into an oncoming truck. How could I have been so arrogant? Surely it had been only a matter of time before passing on curves would catch up with me. And that day was nearly here. I couldn't imagine a world without Manya, and yet I felt like I had been cruel to bring her into such a situation.

But all I could do was drive Karen to radiation treatments and Manya to birthday parties and soccer games, and try to impart psychically, energetically, what I know about passing on curves. Maybe they could succeed where I had failed.

At this point I have to confess that I am still alive. A couple years ago, I drove down to visit Manya at college. She told me all she was up to. She was the founder and president of a campus organization that raises money for poverty-relief projects. Then there were her regular academic classes, evening Swahili classes, ballet, voice, and yoga. And she had just revised her resume for a summer internship in the Congo. I worried about her overdoing it, but she seemed to be holding it together.

Two days later, she texted her mom and me (her mom is still alive, too, but we are no longer together) to say she had accepted a part in a play. Her mother couldn't answer. Her overbooked, overwhelmed daughter was taking on yet one more thing. But I just texted back, "Congratulations." You see, my daughter, like her father, and in some ways like her cancer-survivor mother, doesn't pay enough attention to limitations. She passes on curves.

All I can do is point out the hazard signs and warn her to slow down. And if she drives over the cliff, I will be there to pick her up, clean her off, and put her back on the road. Because that is what a parent does.

Passing on curves is part of who she is. After all, she thrived in a family where both parents expected to die before she left for college. Which begs the question: Which of us was behind the wheel?

And who am I to judge when it comes to passing on curves? I have come to terms with it in myself. It is what I do. It is what I have always done. It is who I am.

Rebecca

HER BROTHER DAVID CALLED and let me know she was dead. Rebecca had been admitted to the hospital because her liver was failing, and while there she had contracted pneumonia. After I got off the phone, I turned off the lights and sat in the dark. I was like an owl hunting mice, but what I was hunting were memories.

When they came, they weren't the ones Rebecca would have feared—no slurred words, no desperate, late-night calls. Instead, I could smell heat lightning and chlorine, hear the sound of a pool motor humming in the backyard, sense the slow shuffle of large dogs rising and settling in the night. And later, on the edge of sleep, I could almost feel the tangle of damp sheets again, the pressure of her thighs, and the weight of her hand on my head.

Rebecca had called unexpectedly during my first Thanksgiving break from college. She was babysitting and wanted to know if I would like to come by. We put the kids to bed and talked. Rebecca told me how an earlier babysitter had invited her boyfriend over and had sex in front of the kids. When the

103

mother and father came home early and caught them in the act, the father had thrown the boyfriend out of the house. I mean that quite literally. The boyfriend had been naked, and the point of exit had been the plate-glass window.

"The kids are still in therapy," Rebecca said.

"Why?" I asked. "Because they saw people having sex or because they saw their father hurl a naked man through a plate-glass window?"

As we were leaving, Rebecca gave me an amazing goodbye kiss—wet, sloppy, warm, her tongue practically reaching down my throat.

It was a secret kiss. I didn't tell anyone, because Rebecca was my stepsister. Technically. We had never slept under the same roof or done much as blended family.

Rebecca was a wild thing. She had a way of commanding the room when she entered, was two years ahead of everyone else her age in school, and was one of the most beautiful women I have ever met, even to this day. She was also sexually precocious. At twelve she had the body of a swimsuit model and began picking up older men in the college library and sneaking them into the house.

Rebecca called again after I got home for Christmas. She was sitting for the same family. When the children were asleep, she opened the liquor cabinet in the den and began drinking straight from a bottle of vodka. We watched television in the den and talked a little, but soon she was asleep.

When the mother came home, she didn't seem to mind finding her sitter asleep beside a depleted vodka bottle and someone else watching her family. When I dropped Rebecca off at my father's house, she promised to call and gave me another one of those kisses, this one richly flavored with vodka and sleep.

A few days later she delivered on her promise. "Your father's gone out," she said as soon as I answered the phone. "I have the place to myself. You want to come over?"

"Yeah."

"Hurry."

Rebecca's room was freezing. She slept with the windows open because it was good for her dogs' coats. She undressed and pulled the covers over her upper body until only her legs and crotch were exposed. I discovered something that night that no one had warned me about growing up—that there is such a thing as bad sex.

"Are you just going to grind away down there all night?" Rebecca asked at last from beneath her covers.

I was happy to stop grinding away if that meant I could crawl under the blankets and get warm.

"You know," said Rebecca. "You and I are a lot alike."

"How so?"

"I don't think either one of us will ever fall in love."

I understood what she was saying, but her comment made me sad, more for her than for me. I was astounded that someone so young could have so much insight—and be so resigned.

We heard the sound of my father's car pulling into the driveway and scrambled into our clothes. I was relieved to have that conversation behind us.

I saw Rebecca off and on over many years when I was in town visiting my family. If neither of us was in a relationship, we would sometimes sleep together. Though I had fallen in love with Rachel, it was true that Rebecca and I were alike in some ways, and unlike our first time together, the sex was often very pleasurable.

The last time I saw her, I picked her up at her condo before taking her to lunch. Her place was packed with large pieces of antique furniture inherited from her grandfather. When I told her I needed to pee, she led me on a twisting path through the maze of furniture. I was honestly afraid I wouldn't be able to find my way back. The toilet bowl was so crusted that I thought twice about using it, even though gas station men's rooms rarely faze me.

Over lunch, she told me she was seeing a new psychiatrist. "He thinks it is ADD. We are trying some new drugs."

When I dropped her off at her place, she asked when she would see me next. Then this once bold woman asked shyly, "Would you like to come up?"

I pictured her place. "No thanks."

"I was thinking, maybe you could talk to your wife, ask her if she would mind if we slept together again. I mean . . . if she said it was OK."

"I am sure she won't go for it," I said.

She nodded. There had been no wantonness in her face during the exchange, only loneliness and need. She climbed out of the car and then ducked her head back through the open window. "Could you ask?" she said. "I would like that."

Rebecca would call from time to time, and the calls became more frequent after my daughter was born. She typically called very late at night, and her speech was always slurred. She would explain that she was tired and had forgotten to account for the time difference.

She would always ask about my daughter. "Tell me again what she looks like? Did you get the sheepskin I sent for her?" One night she broke down sobbing. "Everyone around me is dying," she said. "A friend drove his car into a tree. The old man in the downstairs apartment shot himself last week."

"Don't you see?" she said. "For her to be born now, in the midst of all this death, gives me something to hold onto. It gives me a way to believe in life again. I know she's beautiful. I've never seen her and I know it, just like I know I love her. I love her more than anything in the world. She gives me hope."

My favorite story to tell about Rebecca is how she survived ovarian cancer in her early twenties. Ovarian cancer at such a young age is almost always terminal, but Rebecca was a fighter. One day, she got up from her hospital bed in defiance of her doctor's orders and called a cab to take her to work. She completed her shift with her IV drip hanging from a portable pole. Rebecca offered this story as an example of her tenacity. I received it and shared it with others in the same vein. Looking back, however, it wasn't restlessness or boredom or a need to have a sense of purpose or anything else along those lines that drove her to rise from her apparent death bed and shuffle into work. She was a bartender. She needed a drink.

I can't think of anything sadder than the notion that someone who fought so hard to survive ovarian cancer would then drink herself to death ten years later.

After Rebecca's death, I opened up about our past so that my family could understand what I was going through, but one sister screamed at me in unbridled outrage, "Do you know what it's like to learn that my brother was fucking my stepsister?" I don't know what it was like for her to hear about Rebecca and me, but my sister does not know what it's like to have a relationship that was important and loving, however screwed up it might have been, reduced to a story of perversion and filth.

And she is not the one who for years would wake up in the middle of the night to find Rebecca standing in the corner, looking so sad and empty, looking for me to make things better—and maybe to teach her something about falling in love.

A Disturbance in the Force

ONE MORNING MANY YEARS AGO, I was standing over the sink, getting water for my coffee, when I was overcome by the sudden bout of sobbing: shoulders heaving, unable to fill my lungs, abdominal muscles cramping, random guttural sounds escaping my throat—that kind of sobbing. As my tears splattered in the stainless-steel sink, I tried to figure out where this was coming from. My wife and I had been having a hard time, and work was stressful, but nothing I could think of explained this. I finally composed myself, set up the coffee maker, and went out on the porch to get the newspaper.

A neighbor was walking by and said, "Have you heard?"

"Heard what?"

"Turn on the TV."

I did, just in time to see a plane strike the second tower.

This will sound fantastic to many of you—delusional, grandiose. This is the stuff of movies. How does it go? "I felt a great disturbance in the Force, as if millions of voices suddenly cried out in terror and were suddenly silenced. I fear something terrible has happened." And yet it happened

When I finally pulled myself away from the TV, I remembered the last time I had cried like that. It was May 8, 1996, the night I drove home from the Business Resource Center and Sertoma Bingo Hall in Centralia, Washington. That was the night I understood the scope of another tragedy, one whose death toll was twice that of the World Trade Center attacks.

I am talking about how HIV nearly wiped out the hemophiliacs of my generation. During the 1980s and early 1990s, I buried a lot of friends, some gay friends, a couple former IV drug users, and a lot hemophiliacs. At the time, the hemophilia holocaust, as it was called by people prone to hyperbole, was widely considered to have been unavoidable. People knew we needed meds to survive, and it took the manufacturers time to figure out what was happening and to find a way to produce clean medicine. But then there were the crazies.

I went to the Business Resource Center and Sertoma Bingo Hall to see my friend Corey. We had met when we had shared a hospital room, and we had a lot in common. We were both investigative journalists and held similar political views. He was a news director at Pacifica Radio, and I was a news editor at the San Francisco Bay Guardian. But Corey was one of the angry ones, the ones looking to assign blame. I was too Zen to get caught up in that, but Centralia was near my home and I wanted to say hi.

Corey was there to promote the work of a group he cofounded, the Committee of Ten Thousand. If you took the 7,000 or so infected hemophiliacs in the country and added in sexual partners and infant children, that was the number you came up with. Unfortunately, I had to sit through the paranoia. I should have known better. Corey was a very good investigator, and by the time I left, I was a conspiracy theorist, too.

If you want the full details, you can read Randy Shilts' book, *And the Band Played On*. Here's the thumbnail version: During the 1960s, the drug companies refused to adopt technology that would kill viruses in medicines for hemophiliacs. We all got hepatitis C in the 1970s. The companies wanted blood from people exposed to hepatitis B to make the serum given to travelers, so they collected blood from skid rows, prisons, border towns, and neighborhoods like Christopher Street and the Castro. They weren't supposed to use the hepatitis-infected blood to make our medicine, but they did. They would mix something like 20,000 pints together in a huge vat, pretty much guaranteeing that each batch was contaminated. When they found out that HIV and hep C are transmitted the same way, they didn't act. When the CDC reported the extent of hemophiliac infections, the drug companies' tame watchdog, the FDA, challenged the CDC. And when the companies couldn't deny that their medicine was tainted and finally figured out how to purify it, they sold the contaminated doses overseas.

Each decision could be rationalized, but when I looked at the entire pattern of events, I could only reach one conclusion: The drug companies were willing to watch people die as long as they made their money.

Interstate 5 north of Chehalis is pretty much a straight shot, and the northbound lane was empty at ten o'clock that night. Looking back, I am grateful for both those things, because instead of steering, I was pounding both fists on the top of the wheel. Fortunately, I was also blessed with dry weather. I could barely see the road through an outpouring of tears—rain would have made things that much worse. At one point, driving seventy miles an hour, I lowered my head against the steering wheel for several seconds, closed my eyes, and sobbed.

I should have pulled over, or at least slowed down, but in that moment I didn't really care whether I died.

I rolled down the window to let the cold air dry my tears and yelled to the empty highway. "They tried to kill me. The fucking bastards tried to kill me. They did kill me; I'm just not dead yet. They murdered me for money. They decided that my life didn't matter. They decided I didn't matter. Fucking assholes. Fucking, fucking, fucking assholes."

I was still crying when I walked through my front door forty minutes later.

Over the next few years, I collected stories. About the people infected needlessly, well after the insiders knew what was happening. About the daughter that school officials didn't want in class. About the profoundly sick and disabled man who came to San Francisco to protest outside the law firm that was defending one of the manufacturers against a class-action lawsuit. The lead attorney had once said the best strategy was to "wait them out." The protester tried to talk to that attorney as he was heading toward his car, and the attorney turned and snarled, "Get a job." Eventually, I had to conclude this wasn't simply about cognitive dissonance. It was about greed. It was about immorality.

I don't know exactly what happened to me on the morning of September 11, 2001. Perhaps I was aware of 3,000 lives being extinguished, or maybe I was just picking up on the vibes of my anguished neighbors. But perhaps what set me off was an allergic reaction to the evilness of it all.

I can't speak for Obi-Wan Kenobi, but is it possible the disturbance in the Force wasn't simply about the extinguishing of souls but was also about the full exercise of unmitigated evil? After all, isn't that what Darth Vader represents in the

111

early *Star Wars* episodes, and what the Sith lords represent in later episodes?

When I was crying, driving blind, on my way home from Chehalis, I had already buried my friends. I had already mourned my own death. That wasn't the source of my pain. What set me off wasn't grief; it was the sure and certain knowledge that here, now, on this very planet, the Sith lords walk among us.

The Porky Beast

MY DAUGHTER WOKE FROM A BAD DREAM one night, and my wife brought her into our bed to sleep. In the morning, I asked Manya to tell me about the nightmare.

"We were out playing in the backyard—you, me, and Mommy—and there was a scary animal. It was in the tall grass by the fence."

"What kind of animal?"

"It wasn't a real animal. It was porky, and I think it had a big tail."

"Porky?"

Karen, who had heard about the dream in the night, translated for me: "It had spines. Like a porcupine."

The simple expressiveness of Manya's dreams has always amazed me. Several months earlier, Manya had awoken from another bad dream. "You were walking down the street," she told me tearfully. "I kept calling your name, but you wouldn't turn around. You just kept walking away from me." I felt exposed by that dream. Without telling my wife or my daughter,

I had quietly begun to investigate homes for sale in the neighborhood. I was looking for something small, just enough room for one adult and a part-time child.

The porky beast first appeared in 1997 as dust specks on a mammogram. Microcalcifications, ductal carcinoma in situ. Too pervasive for a lumpectomy. One surgeon took the breast, and then another surgeon built a new one out of belly fat and muscle. The pathology report was good. Clean margins, no invasive cells. But two years later, Karen awoke with a painful lump under her arm, and the same surgeon who had removed her breast performed a biopsy.

He called in the middle of dinner the next day. Karen shook her head as she listened—a subtle movement but enough to confirm what I had learned at the hospital.

"It was a lot bigger than I expected," the surgeon had told me when Karen was in the recovery room. "And very hard."

"Hard? That's not good is it?"

"No. I only removed two, but there were several others in there."

"That were enlarged?"

"Yes. And hard."

When Karen got off the phone, she told Manya and me that the doctors had found cancer. For several minutes, it looked like she was going to maintain her composure. But when I began to explain what cancer was to Manya, Karen got up and staggered into the den, where she had been sleeping since her surgery. Manya followed, asking questions Karen couldn't answer, and Karen in her pain and fear turned to Manya and sobbed, "This is serious, Manya. People can die from this." The two of them crawled under the covers. They clenched and cried and cried some more. "This can't be happening," said Karen. "I have Manya."

Karen spent most of the next couple of days in bed. She watched a lot of bad TV and worked her way through *Harry Potter and the Sorcerer's Stone*. Once, while walking through the living room, she paused, and her arms began to shake uncontrollably. A few days later, though, she was up and about. A small sticky note appeared on the wall beside the bathroom mirror: "Be positive."

Karen had three months of chemo, and then surgery to remove her lymph nodes. Chances of surviving breast cancer are tied to the number of positive lymph nodes. Back then, having ten or more positive nodes was considered a bad sign. Today it is even fewer. Between the two surgeries, Karen had more than fifty positive nodes removed from her armpit and the shoulder on one side. Some people don't have that many on both sides combined. I called a friend, a doctor married to a doctor, and posed this question: What would you say about this case if you were just talking about it over dinner? She consulted with her oncology colleagues and came back with an answer: two years to recurrence and another two until death.

I had been house hunting because I felt that Karen had become increasingly distant. Of course, as my mother often said when we kids were squabbling, it takes two to tango, and I was equally responsible for our problems. Karen could never tell me definitively why she kept retreating; in fact, she told me she didn't know herself.

I decided that there were lots of reasons—our relationship was incredibly complex—but that part of the problem was that I had overstayed my welcome. I already had HIV when we met, and we decided to have a kid with the expectation that Karen would become a single parent. Neither one of us had foreseen a future together that extended beyond a few years.

We had never talked about growing old together. We had never imagined it as an ideal.

So, I kept waiting for the morning when Karen would wake up and turn to me and ask, "Are you still here?"

When I told Karen about this notion, she told me it wasn't true. In fact, she was horrified. I don't want to leave the impression that she wanted me to die. I am sure she didn't. But all relationships are some part fantasy. Ours was a dark fantasy. Karen's destiny was to become the romantic survivor. But I hadn't stayed in character, and now we were off-script and floundering when it came to shaping a new narrative.

Maybe Karen was right, maybe my theory was ridiculous, but after her diagnosis, I came to believe in it even more, because now the roles were reversed. My new HIV meds seemed to be working, and now I expected to become a single parent. I tried to support Karen as much as I could and was reminded of how much I loved her, regardless of the state of our marriage. But to be honest—and I am not proud of this—I began to imagine a life without Karen, one where I was free to follow my own impulses, to start over in a relationship that wasn't bogged down by a history of hardship. Only Karen didn't follow the script, either. Like me, she survived.

So, what do you do with a marriage like this? One where first one partner and then the other was expected to die, and neither of us ever planned on growing old together? Where neither of us wanted the other to die, but we could both imagine a level of freedom and a certain amount of relief if it happened? Where there were days when dying somehow seemed like the "right" answer?

Well, we took a lesson from our daughter. The night she came into our bed frightened by the porky beast, between the time she settled in with us and the time she fell back asleep,

116

Manya worked to transform the thing that had terrified her. She told me in the morning that she had "turned it into something friendly."

And that's what Karen and I did. It was hard work. It took years. When we were both able to admit we were no longer romantic partners, we talked to Manya first, and then to our family and friends. We stayed together for a couple years as friends, co-parents, economic partners, and housemates. When I reconnected with Rachel, I moved out, and we worked slowly through that difficult transition.

Our finances are still intertwined. We participate in the same social groups. I sometimes stay at the old house when I visit, especially if Manya is in town. We all wake up together on Christmas mornings and re-create our family rituals. And if one of us were ever to get seriously ill again, the other one would be there to help.

Don't get me wrong: It was often painful. There were long stretches of shouting and even longer stretches of silence. But in the end we chose the only way open to us if we wanted to be good parents and good role models for Manya:

Like I said, we turned it into something friendly.

Burning Toast

WHEN KAREN WAS UNDERGOING chemotherapy, she was too tired to help out around the house or do much with Manya. I felt like a single parent, the family breadwinner, and a medical caregiver all at once. So I was glad one morning when Karen said she was feeling better and offered to drive Manya to school before going to a meeting.

Karen had a pile of things to take with her, and Manya had her usual items—a sweater, a lunch bag, a small backpack—but it was the week our family was responsible for providing afternoon snacks for Manya's second-grade class, so we had two plastic shopping bags that had to go to school. One contained four boxes of chocolate-chip granola bars; the other, fourteen recently halved bananas.

Karen said she needed help getting everything to the car, and Manya began to load up. She poked her arms through the two straps of the backpack and positioned it, then she settled the strap of her lunch bag over her head and across her shoulder. As I reached for one of the shopping bags, Manya firmly said, "No."

Before Karen's diagnosis, we would have considered ourselves lucky if Manya had carried her own stuff to the car, but now she had a strong need to help. "I want to do it all," she said, and I let her.

As Manya struggled down the front walk, I thought, "Such a heavy burden for a child so young." And I didn't mean her various bags.

Later that day, I received an e-mail from my friend Hilary. She was asking how I was doing. "Mostly I'm OK," I wrote back, "but this morning is particularly hard. I just want to cry and eat cinnamon rolls."

"I always felt like I could just check out if the HIV or hepatitis got bad," I told Hilary. "Now I don't have that option, even if Karen recovers. The threat of a recurrence is always there, so I have to fight. I'm tired, Hilary. Life sucks, and I'm tired of having to rise to the occasion. I don't want Manya to have to learn to be tough like I have done, but I know her, and that's what she'll do if it comes down to it. Sometimes I think I should fall apart just so she knows she has options."

Hilary answered almost immediately. "If there ever was a time to fall apart, this would be it. Try it, you have friends nearby. Perhaps our children need to see the edifice of adulthood crumble. I wish I was there to give you a hug and feed you cinnamon rolls."

She went on to ask, "What would breaking down look like for you?"

The truth is, I had no idea. I have never bounced a check, much less suffered a nervous collapse. In my twenties, my sense of responsibility troubled me so much that I once spent an entire morning teaching myself how to burn toast, with limited success.

119

Manya had already shouldered the burden of character, and I was afraid that she was destined for a lifetime of trying to pull other people's toast out of the fire.

I recognized this because I, too, have character. I say that humbly. It's not something I'm proud of. It is just something that comes with growing up with a chronic health condition and not wanting to be a burden. I have come to see character as a weakness as well as a strength.

A few months later, Manya came home from school in a cranky mood. Normally a pleasant, compliant child, she was surly. She complained about everything, like the food I served for dinner. She threw a fit when I told her it was bedtime. In the morning, she was slow to get ready. And at one point she said she didn't want to go to school. This from a child who always loved school.

Finally, I sat her down at the dining room table. "This kind of behavior is not like you," I said, keeping my voice low so Karen wouldn't hear us in the den. "Can you tell me what is really going on?"

Manya looked at me for a moment, looked in the direction of the den where her mother was recuperating from the latest round of chemo, and then went into the kitchen to get a pen. When she came back, she started writing something on the corner of the newspaper. She kept her hand cupped around the pen so I couldn't see what she was writing. Then she tore off the corner and handed it to me. It read, "I want to die!"

I can't tell you exactly what happened after that because I can't remember. I think I was in a state of shock. I do know that we both cried quietly. We talked a little in whispers. I tried to console her. And eventually we agreed she would go to school. I think just getting it out there made her feel better.

From what she told me, and what I was later able to get from talking to the teachers and other parents, I was able to piece together what had happened. The day before, the school had learned that the mother of one of the students had committed suicide, and the teachers had decided to talk to the kids about grief. In Manya's class, kids had shared their stories about death. One of the kids had talked about two pet mice that had died of cancer, and this had prompted another student to talk about her grandfather. The school had known about Manya's situation at home, but the teachers hadn't made the connection. They hadn't thought to call us and let us know what had taken place.

I took that torn-off corner of the newspaper and had it laminated the same day, and then I stuck it in my wallet. Every day at work for the next few months, at least once a day, I would close the door to my office, take the paper out of my wallet and stare at it. And I would cry for five or ten minutes at a time. It was a reminder to never take what Manya was going through for granted just because she seemed to be holding up on the outside. But after the first few weeks, I realized that my ritual was about more than just Manya. It was also about me. It was a chance for me to grieve over my own situation, to acknowledge that there were days I wanted to die.

Hilary was right: Sometimes it is a gift to our children to let them see the edifice of adulthood crumble. But Manya allowed me to see the edifice of childhood crumble.

That was her gift to me.

Fractured Truths

I WENT BACK TO THE TIGER FARM to see Mike in 1996. He was dying. When he staggered out of the house to see me, his labored, unsteady steps carried him across the porch where my mother first spotted Engels the tiger after his escape and toward two lounge chairs sitting in the dirt yard. I could remember my mother replacing their tattered woven webbing. One chaise was in roughly the spot where Mike had stood when he had swung his steel-toed boot at Jason the wolfhound after the rambunctious puppy had grabbed a turkey drumstick from his hand. The other was in roughly the spot where Jason had collapsed abruptly.

In my day, the farm had been the private zoo of an eccentric biologist, a place known simply as the farm; when I returned, it was a bona fide nonprofit known as the Carnivore Preservation Trust. But it seemed as if the modern story of a credible international organization dedicated to species preservation had been written on used parchment from which the past had supposedly been scraped away, and yet traces of the old story, the story I had witnessed, still peeked through.

The farm was a palimpsest.

Mike had always been so robust, so vigorous, and my eyes started to tear when I saw him like that, weak and vulnerable because of the cancer. This is the man I once saw, calm as you please, deliver a full roundhouse kick to the nose of an advancing Bengal tiger.

His partner Kay, the woman who replaced my mother, was fiercely protective at first and insisted that I not disturb Mike. "The interferon gives him incredible fevers," she told me. "We have to have him stand in an ice-cold shower to cool him down or he will die."

Kay either did not understand, or refused to acknowledge, that Mike was a second father to me, and it was not just an affectation when Mike referred to me as "son."

Knowing he would want to see me, I had insisted that she ask him, and he came outside as I knew he would. Kay helped Mike settle into the nearest chaise, and I sat in the other. "I am not afraid of dying," he said. "But there is so much I have to do before I go. The interferon can buy me a little time at least. I need to finish the transition planning."

I had been living on the West Coast for fifteen years, but I visited Mike almost every time I went home to see the rest of the family. I was the only one in my family who regularly stopped by. Mike had remained important to me in ways I have never been able to capture. Every time I get close to articulating why, the words flit away like gibbons swinging through the forest canopy. I do know that whenever he asked me how I was doing, he stopped to listen to my answer. Sometimes he made comments that let me know he thought about who I was, actually saw me. And he never treated me differently because of my hemophilia.

Still, these visits were hard. Mike would invariably steer the conversation around to his volunteer work as a domestic-violence counselor. And when he did, I remembered his hand rising to strike my mother, heard him shout again, "Keep going, son, if you know what's good for you." I know where most of the counselors for these programs come from, but Mike never used the term *peer counselor*. He never mentioned his own tendency toward violence, and he never came within a tiger's whisker of apologizing.

These conversations also brought to mind the day Mike shot one of the goats.

In my memory of the event, Mike had taken his time. One shot to the heart. I was amazed that the shell from the hunting rifle, his prized Weatherby .300, had entered so cleanly. A small, red hole had flowered briefly on the goat's white coat before the animal had toppled.

"A compassionate kill," Mike had said to the knot of men outside the cage. As if it wasn't him who had put the goat in the tiger's cage in the first place, just to see if his hand-raised pet could kill efficiently. As if it hadn't been him who stood, Weatherby resting on his muscled shoulder, watching as the tiger played with the goat the way a house cat might play with a mouse, seemingly immune to the terrified bleating and the smell when the tiger had surgically opened up the goat's side.

A compassionate kill? More like a compassionate lie, a fractured, fragmented sliver of truth, as if all Mike had to view himself with was a shard of a broken mirror.

I can't recall for sure: As Mike sat in the chaise, the kidney cancer devouring his body, did I tell him I loved him? I don't think so. I am pretty sure I only thought it, did not speak it, because

I was afraid to voice my own fractured truth. I did love him, but if I had said, "I hate you," it would be just another shard from the same irreparably broken mirror. I know I didn't tell him that I had been horrified when he had grinned at the bleating goat. I did not say that I will be forever ashamed that I had left when he told me to, or that I know that if I had turned to confront him, he might have killed me just like he had killed his beloved Jason.

I had no more capacity to say such things than he had to apologize. For too much of my life, I denied the boy who knew such things, felt such things, who held those fragments of the truth. That boy did not go with me into the world. I was ashamed of him, and so I left him behind, caged in a farmhouse with a tiger of a man whom I both loved and hated. And sometimes I tried to pretend that boy was gone, as if I had killed him by my own hand and then turned and said to no one, or to anyone who would listen, "A compassionate kill."

Two weeks after my visit, Mike was dead at the age of fifty-eight. The following Sunday, hundreds gathered at the farm to remember him and to sing his praises. I mourned him from three thousand miles away.

And I read the obituaries and online tributes. I could quibble with the biographical details, but I could not argue with the sentiments of the mourners. They describe a brave, courageous, committed man who followed his convictions.

"He was a nice fellow," a neighbor told the Raleigh paper. "You'd just love to talk to him. He loved his animals, I'll tell you that."

Memorial sites popped up on the Internet. One man posted Michael's entire curriculum vitae online as a tribute, oblivious to the fact that the CV wasn't always accurate. It said Mike had quit teaching to start the nonprofit, for example, when he had actually been denied tenure. The man said Mike "will be a continuing inspiration to those who knew him."

On another site, a former volunteer described him as brilliant, crazy, and eccentric. She mentioned his mood swings and constantly changing priorities. But she also said, "The obvious fact was that this charismatic man cared deeply for the animals, and he loved life."

I liked reading about what was true for these people, because it was true for me, too. But Mike was a complex man, and I hold other truths, truths his fan base will not like.

Much later, I read an Internet posting that mentioned how much Mike loved Lolita, the chimpanzee. I thought of that large, intelligent creature living in a tiny iron cube. I remembered the sadness in her eyes, and the way the padlocked tow chain had chafed off the hair around her neck. Yes, I can agree that Mike loved Lolita very much, but only because I have grown to appreciate, to relish even, how much complexity and ambiguity love can hold.

In an e-mail, Mike's daughter, Anne, now an accomplished attorney and death penalty opponent, wrote "I miss my daddy."

I know, Anne; I miss him, too.

126

What Makes Us Human

THIRTY-SIX YEARS AFTER MEPHISTO the llama crashed into me, I had my knee replaced. It had reached the point where I was unable to stand straight because my leg was permanently bent. My father flew across the country to take care of me after the surgery. He knows I have a hard time accepting help, so he didn't ask; he just called and told me when he was coming.

After two weeks in bed, I was feeling weaker by the day. I had hoped to lose weight after the surgery, but my body was just swapping muscle for fat. When I leaned forward to retrieve a book from the end of the bed, my father said, "You have a really big stomach. I think you get that from your mother's side. She always did have legs like a fullback."

Ever since I audited Mike's evolutionary biology class in high school, I have been intrigued by the question of what makes us human, what about us most saliently distinguishes us from other animals. Most people are familiar with one of the early and now discredited theories, that only humans are tool-users. After that theory was put to rest, it was replaced by a variant. If man the tool user didn't cut it, what about man the toolmaker? Jane Goodall's observations that chimpanzees shape sticks before using them to fish termites from their mounds quashed that notion.

A later concept was that only humans domesticate other animals. Chico and Paco the squirrel monkeys refuted this theory when they rode around on the backs of the pygmy goats.

At one point I entertained the belief that only humans have an awareness of death. Animals have survival drives, but avoiding death is not the same as being aware of it conceptually. The circumstances of Tief's death ended that line of inquiry for me. Tief did not come home to fight for survival; Tief wanted to die at home, and he wanted to say good-bye.

For a while, I followed a discussion in the research literature about whether animals were capable of empathy, which is considered a prerequisite for morality. Tief's ability to find and comfort anyone who was upset at the farm confirmed that animals have empathy, as did Arnie coming out of the basement to comfort me when I was telling the story of Tief's death.

Then there was the notion that only humans lie. Deception is common among animals, but when is deception a lie, and when is it learned behavior? In my mind, a true lie requires something more than an instinctive or reflexive use of trickery. It also requires some level of invention, some way in which the deception is fitted to a particular set of circumstances.

My favorite example of inventive lying is a story Mike told about his wolfhounds, Darwin and Lilly. Mike had given each dog a bone from the butcher. Lilly decided she liked Darwin's better, but every time she approached to take his away, he would snarl and drive her back. Lilly pondered this for a while and then returned to her bone, which she began to guard jealously. She slathered, she snarled, she snapped her teeth in

Darwin's direction. Of course, this made Darwin wonder what was so special about Lilly's bone. He eventually exercised his prerogative as the alpha male to claim Lilly's bone. Lilly surrendered after a half-hearted defense and then went to get Darwin's discarded bone, which she had wanted all along.

In short, animals lie.

I eventually settled on the idea that only humans are capable of self-deception; only they can lie to themselves. I came to this cynical view after I realized that the infection of so many hemophiliacs with HIV had been avoidable. Each step of the way, the manufacturers offered up reasons for their dubious choices. It was possible to accept each excuse individually, but in the end, every choice was wrong, and every choice aligned with what would make the most money. I truly believe that the executives couldn't accept that they were the kind of people who would risk killing people in the name of profit, so they made up stories again and again, until what they had was a long, tragic narrative. It wasn't a lie exactly—more of a self-deluding bedtime story that helped them sleep at night.

My father's presence at my bedside, however, suggested there was something more. Yes, humans are uniquely capable of self-deception, but for good and for ill, they are also capable of more.

My father is retired and still lives in Chapel Hill. For a long time, my only contact with him was when I went home or when a business trip took him through wherever I was living. We saw each other very little, and the time we did spend together was tense.

During a period in which I was writing poems and thinking a lot about poetry, I recalled looking for his copy of *The Joy of Sex* as a kid and coming across some handwritten poems in his desk drawer. I had had no idea that he wrote poetry. This memory came to represent everything he had ever withheld from me, and the more I thought about it, the angrier I became. I wrote a vicious poem about him and mailed it without comment, thinking we might never talk again.

But he thanked me in a letter. He wrote, "I no longer feel like I have to cry every time I hear Harry Chapin's 'Cat's in the Cradle.'" He enclosed some of his poems, including some very tender ones about me.

Since then, things have been easier, and I understand him better. When I was in the seventh grade, for example, I was crying, and he slapped me. He told me, "Men don't cry." I now know he had been bullied as a child, and he was afraid that if I showed weakness I might be beaten and die from my injuries.

So, when he told me I had a big stomach and went on to say that he was only concerned about the extra weight I would carry on my post-surgery knee, part of me wanted to forgive him. But his reference to my mother's legs got to me. Occasionally, my mother has opened up about the early years of their marriage, and high on her long list of remembered slights is the time my father told her she had legs like a fullback. When I heard the same words from my father's mouth, I remembered how my mother had cried when she had told me that story years before.

The irony is that I am built like my father, barrel-chested and squat. We carry our weight up top, not in our legs. In fact, my legs are severely atrophied after all my injuries. The notion that my mother's legs—which look nothing like the legs of a fullback, by the way—are the hereditary source of my gut is totally absurd.

I wanted to yell this at my father. I wanted to defend my mother. But I stayed quiet. No matter how insensitive my father was being about my stomach and my mother's legs, I also had to contend with this simple set of facts: I was in pain. I couldn't walk more than a few feet. I couldn't easily fend for myself. And my father was the person sitting by my bedside day after day.

As a child, it would have been my mother, never him, but he had recast his story. He had chosen to become the person who would fly 3,000 miles to be at my bedside. He had chosen to become my father.

We humans are capable of self-deception, but we are also uniquely capable of self-conception. We are constantly shaping and reshaping ourselves, telling and retelling our stories. I fictionalized my sexual autobiography. Rachel left me in search of a story of self that she could inhabit comfortably. Mike revised his history around violence. Rebecca redacted her drinking when she was in my presence.

We humans are complicated. Our personalities are layered—accretions of various ids, egos, superegos, personas, alter egos, ego-ideals, higher selves, unconscious selves, imaginal selves, past selves, and inner children. Animals are different. Animals are what they are. If they deceive you, it is because they are fulfilling their fundamental nature.

We big-brained apes, however, use story, including fiction, to make sense of all our contradictions, to make ourselves more comfortable with our messy, complicated humanness. We breathe life into those stories to animate them, and then we send our self-representations out into the world like avatars.

Humans can disassemble and dissemble, it's true, but we can also reassemble. And if we are lucky, we can eventually, through an iterative process of disassembly and reassembly, come to resemble our true selves.

So perhaps this is what makes us human: story.
We are all our own editors. We are all storytellers.

Notes on Form

WHEN I WAS A JOURNALIST, there was a move to break away from the traditional news article structure (the reverse pyramid) and to teach reporters how to tell stories. When I worked for a college and we needed to recruit more applicants, everyone said the solution was to do a better job of telling the college's story. When I worked in public health, government kept cutting public health funding, and the public had no idea what public health did, so everyone in the field frantically cast about for ways to tell "the story of public health."

At a very basic level, humans grasp the importance of story, but we sometimes have trouble identifying what makes a story a story and, in particular, what makes a story a good story. That's because stories are everywhere and take a seemingly infinite number of forms.

We sometimes have the same difficulty trying to define storytelling. It is an amazingly broad concept. In cafes and bars and living rooms, we all tell stories. Fiction writers write stories, and they often read their stories aloud; that is, they tell them. Go to a gathering of professional storytellers, and you may find one person enthusiastically reading a children's book over here and another person dramatically recounting an ancient myth over there. The list of performers who are, to one degree or another, storytellers is long indeed: monologists, solo performers, spoken-word artists, and stand-up comics, to name a few.

There is a particular form of storytelling, however, that is wildly popular these days and takes a readily identifiable form. I am talking about the kind of personal storytelling that occurs on radio programs like *The Moth* and *Snap Judgment* and at dozens if not hundreds of local venues around the country. The rules differ from program to program and venue to venue, but the general requirements are:

• The story must be true.

• The recounted events must be from the storyteller's own life (not generic stories, urban myths, or stories about something that happened to someone the storyteller knows).

• The presentation must feel spontaneous (not like it is part of a carefully rehearsed routine).

• To encourage a spontaneous feel, the storyteller must work without scripts or notes.

• The story must be tellable within a fixed time limit (often five or ten minutes).

The formats for personal storytelling events and programs tend to be pretty consistent, but they can vary in some ways. Fireside Storytelling, one of several popular events in San Francisco, convenes the first Wednesday of each month. Six invited storytellers are allowed ten, maybe fifteen minutes each. There is a different theme each month. Across the Bay in Oakland, The Shout convenes on the second Monday. Its organizers hold a little firmer to the ten-minute limit, and audience members can put their names in a hat for a chance to tell a six-minute story between the longer stories. The Shout doesn't use themes. Down the coast in Santa Cruz, Word Up! does not follow a regular schedule, and the producers mix ten-minute personal storytelling with longer, slicker solo performance pieces. The producers at *Snap Judgment* want pieces that are about eight minutes long. On-air pieces for *The Moth* can run a little longer, but one of the judging criteria for its live StorySlams is that the stories don't exceed five minutes. And *Risk* wants stories you would normally tell only to your therapist.

Each of the personal essays in this collection is intended to do double duty as a script for live personal storytelling, although *template* might be a better word than *script*, because no story will be told exactly the same way twice. A ten-minute story works out to be 1,500 words maximum, which is equivalent to four to six double-spaced pages or a Microsoft Word file of around 20 megabytes. That is why every essay here is 1,300 to 1,500 words.

Because these stories are meant to be fluid, altering them to fit a particular set of circumstances is easy and guilt-free. For this collection, I have edited out explanations of things the reader will already know from the preceding essays. I don't have to constantly repeat that Mike was a biology professor, say, or that Tief was my dog. And if a vignette or an anecdote would normally appear in more than one story, I have chosen which one to include it in for this book. That way, the stories wouldn't seem too repetitive if read as a group.

For live performances, I restore those details. If I have to work with a shorter time slot, I will edit something out (chances are I will already have a good sense of what I can cut). I also might refer to something another performer said, bring in a current event, try to tie the piece more closely to the evening's theme if there is one, or improvise somehow based on my sense of the audience. If you read the essays in print and then listen to one of my recordings or a live performance, don't be surprised if they don't match word for word.

Endnotes

THE EPIGRAPH IS AN excerpt from "All the Bodies," a poem by Ruth L. Schwartz that appears in *Miraculum* (Autumn House Press, 2012).

"The Blue Flute" was first performed on Sept. 21, 2013, at The Abbey in Santa Cruz.

"A Different Kind of Injury" was first performed at Fireside Storyteling in San Francisco (date unknown).

"Role Model" and "More Human than Most People" were first performed on Aug. 6, 2014, at Fireside Storytelling in San Francisco.

"Jason and the Hells Angels" was first performed on Feb. 11, 2013, at The Shout in Oakland.

"Lolita the Chimp" was first performed on Jan. 9, 2013, at Fireside Storytelling in San Francisco.

"Jeff the Bear" was first performed Sept. 23, 2013, at The Marsh in San Francisco.

"No Longer a Virgin" was first performed January 8, 2014, at Fireside Storytelling in San Francisco.

"The Porn Store" was first performed on Sept. 4, 2013, at Fireside Storytelling in San Francisco.

"Role Model," was first performed on Aug. 6, 2014, at Fireside Storytelling in San Francisco.

"He Makes Me Laugh" was first performed Feb. 28, 2013, at Coyote Crossing in Santa Cruz.

"Uncle Mack's Passing" was first performed at Fireside Storytelling in San Francisco (date unknown).

"The Cloak of Nessus" was first performed Feb. 6, 2013, at Fireside Storytelling in San Francisco.

"The Fox Demon" was first performed May 13, 2013, at The Shout in Oakland.

"Passing on Curves" was first performed Dec. 5, 2012, at Fireside Storytelling in San Francisco.

"Rebecca," was first performed on Sept. 26, 2013, at TMI in Berkeley.

"A Disturbance in the Force" was first performed Feb. 6, 2013, at Fireside Storytelling in San Francisco.

"Burning Toast" was first performed April 26, 2013, at Word Up! in Santa Cruz.

"What Makes Us Human" was first performed on Aug. 21, 2013, at La Mariposa in Masaya, Nicaragua.

Acknowledgments

THIS BOOK IS DEDICATED TO MY DAUGHTER Manya because of her patience and her faith in me.

I want to thank all the people who have contributed to my development as a writer. I have been blessed with too many teachers and mentors to name them all here, but in particular I want to acknowledge Olivia Archibald, Tim Redmond, Ruth L. Schwartz, and Jane Vanderburgh (with the usual caveat that the shortcomings of my own work should not reflect badly on them). I especially want to recognize Ruth Schwartz for inspiring me to write, and for teaching me a great deal about generosity and compassion.

To Karen, thank you for being my courageous partner in parenting, survival, and so many other adventures. It has truly been an amazing ride.

Since the essays in this book are meant to be performance pieces, I have to thank Jen Ryle at Olympia Family Theater for casting me in my first community-theater production. I am profoundly indebted to storytelling venues that allowed me to perform, particularly The Marsh and Fireside Storytelling in San Francisco, The Shout in Oakland, and Word Up! and Lucid Storytelling in Santa Cruz.

Such venues wouldn't exist without the avid fans who support personal storytelling. I am forever grateful for the audience members who have laughed and cried with me during my performances, cheered when I was done (for good reasons, I hope), and approached me afterward to say kind words. This book exists for them and because of them.

CRAIG MCLAUGHLIN is a journalist, essayist, and storyteller. He appears frequently at storytelling venues throughout the country, and particularly in the San Francisco Bay Area where he resides. A former editor of the *San Francisco Bay Guardian*, he has won numerous awards as an investigative reporter, news editor, and memoirist. He has also taught creative nonfiction as an adjunct faculty member at The Evergreen State College and co-authored a graduate-level textbook, *Health Policy Analysis: An Interdisciplinary Approach*. He holds a Master of Journalism degree from the University of California, Berkeley and a Bachelor of Arts in biology from Wesleyan University. Learn more about him and see his performance schedule at www.cdmclaughlin.com. You can also follow him on Twitter at @CraigDMcL and like him on Facebook at www.facebook.com/craigdavidmclaughlin.

CPSIA information can be obtained
at www.ICGtesting.com
Printed in the USA
FSOW02n1204130715
8821FS